Penguin 🐧 Readers

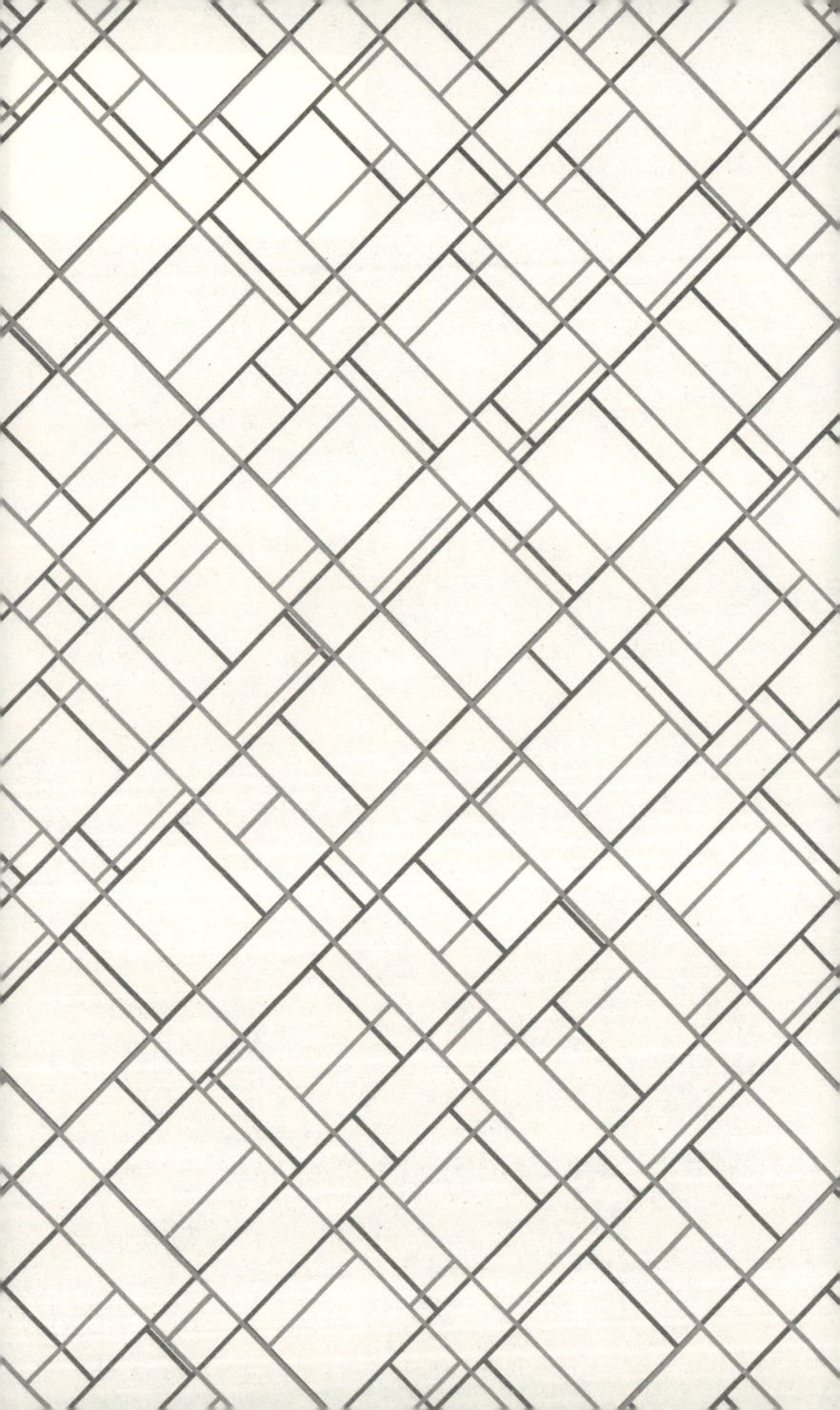

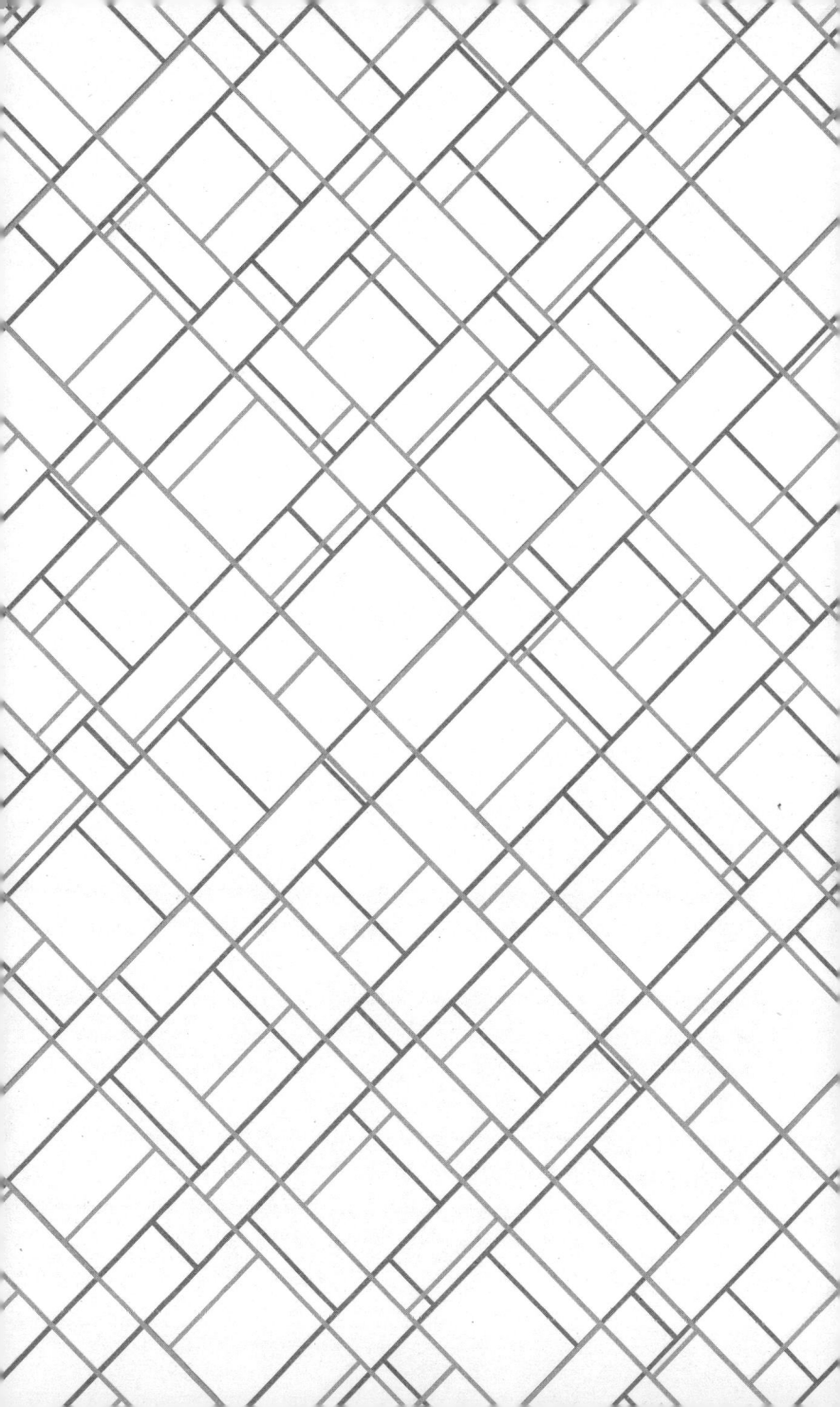

Penguin  Readers

WORK REMOTELY

ANASTASIA TOHMÉ AND
MARTIN WORNER

LEVEL

ADAPTED BY CATRIN MORRIS
SERIES EDITOR: SORREL PITTS

Many of the quotes in this book have been simplified
for learners of English as a foreign language.

PENGUIN BOOKS

UK | USA | Canada | Ireland | Australia
India | New Zealand | South Africa

Penguin Books is part of the Penguin Random House group of companies
whose addresses can be found at global.penguinrandomhouse.com.
www.penguin.co.uk www.puffin.co.uk www.ladybird.co.uk

Work Remotely first published by Penguin General, 2021
This Penguin Readers edition published by Penguin Books Ltd, 2023
001

Original text written by Anastasia Tohmé and Martin Worner
Text for Penguin Readers edition adapted by Catrin Morris
Original copyright © Anastasia Tohmé and Martin Worner
Text copyright © Penguin Books Ltd, 2023
Cover image copyright © Creative Lab/Shutterstock
Design project management by Dynamo Limited

The moral right of the original authors has been asserted

Printed and bound in Great Britain by Clays Ltd, Elcograf S.p.A.

The authorized representative in the EEA is Penguin Random House Ireland,
Morrison Chambers, 32 Nassau Street, Dublin D02 YH68.

A CIP catalogue record for this book is available from the British Library

ISBN: 978-0-241-58916-8

All correspondence to:
Penguin Books
Penguin Random House Children's
One Embassy Gardens, 8 Viaduct Gardens,
London SW11 7BW

Penguin Random House is committed to a
sustainable future for our business, our readers
and our planet. This book is made from Forest
Stewardship Council® certified paper.

Contents

Note about the book	8
Before-reading questions	8
Introduction – Why work remotely?	9
Chapter One – Working in a remote team	14
Chapter Two – Communicating in a remote team	21
Chapter Three – Meeting in a remote team	27
Chapter Four – Managing a remote team	34
Chapter Five – Managing goals and performance	41
Chapter Six – Decision-making, mediation and progression	48
Chapter Seven – Hiring employees	56
Chapter Eight – Self-care	63
Chapter Nine – Wellbeing	71
Chapter Ten – Reaching out	74
Chapter Eleven – Finding balance	80
Conclusion – The future of remote working	86
During-reading questions	88
After-reading questions	90
Exercises	91
Project work	96
Glossary	97
References	105

Note about the book

Martin Worner used to work for **finance*** and technology businesses, before starting his own company, **specializing** in technology for banks and other **financial organizations**. He has worked with **teams** around the world and was quick to move to **remote** working. Today, he is head of **product** at Confio.

Anastasia Tohmé is a **human resources** (HR) **specialist**, she is **responsible** for **hiring** the best people for Safeguard Global, an important world **services** company. She also teaches at Geneva Business School. She lives in Spain and has been fully remote since 2018.

This book looks at the positive and negative sides of working **remotely** for **employees**, managers and companies. It explores **productivity** and people's work–life balance.

Before-reading questions

1 What do you think "working remotely" is?
2 When and why did more people start working remotely, do you think?
3 What is good about working remotely? What is bad about it?

*Definitions of words in **bold** can be found in the glossary on pages 97–104.

INTRODUCTION
Why work remotely?

Since the birth of the modern office, few people have worked **remotely**. A 2018 **survey** found that only 3% of **employees** in the United States of America worked from home more than half of the time. But, since the start of the **coronavirus pandemic** in 2020, thousands of companies have had to close offices and many millions of people have had to work from home. In April 2020, almost 50% of UK employees began to work away from the office. Companies all over the world are now welcoming **remote** working. While he was at Twitter, Jack Dorsey made all jobs remote, except for those that need you to be in an office. Many more companies have followed.

To get the most out of remote work, we need to look at what the **workplace** means and understand what **flexible** work can bring. We need to become more **innovative**, and carefully and actively experiment with different ways of working. Remote work has become the new normal. And it is here to stay.

But why should we do it?
Without the **limits** of an office, many employers can employ people who do not live in the area. In one survey, 64% of employers said that they would probably **hire** remote employees, while most found that **virtual**

hiring was a cheaper way to get good new employees. Companies can use the money that they do not spend on renting offices to pay employees more. Employees are not **limited** to one place, so they can develop a **career** while still staying close to family and friends. According to one survey, people want $24,000 more if you ask them to move away from family.

Remote working also gives the same chances to people whose age, **race**, class, sex or **disability** can make career **development** more difficult. Taking away the cost and need to travel to work every day can really help people who find it difficult or impossible to get to an office. Once in the virtual **workspace**, employees from different groups are treated more fairly, one survey found, because the employer sees the results, not the people.

Several surveys have shown what most of us already knew: working at home increases our **productivity**. In a survey of over 13,000 businesses around the world, 85% found that **teams** were more **productive** when working remotely.[1]

For many employees, working from home means that they have greater **flexibility** and **independence** to plan their day. They have more time for interests, for spending time with family and friends, and for looking after pets. With hours saved by not travelling, workers can spend more time exercising and preparing healthier meals. One survey found that 77% of employees thought that they were healthier and had better **wellbeing** by working from home. In a KBC Bank survey, 87% of people said they had better work–life balance; 83% said that they could **concentrate** more at work; 72% felt less **stressed** at work; 68% were more **motivated**; and 62% could manage their work better.[2] The survey also showed that it was good for employers, too, as there was a 76% increase in employees staying in their jobs when they could work **flexibly**.

Virtual **communication** has also changed the way people see each other in companies. It can be positive to see company managers in their homes on a Zoom call. We see that they, too, have families, homes to manage and their own problems. Many companies welcome this move towards a more human way of managing a company.

Big offices in tall glass buildings in city centres cost companies millions every year. In New York, offices cost about $14,800 per employee every year, with cleaning, food and drinks, and **taxes**.[3] Saving money in this way means that companies can find better employees and pay them more, or buy new technology.

Working from home can also be good for the environment. In 2015, the company Xerox found that its remote workers drove 92,000,000 fewer miles.[4]

Of course, there are still people who are unsure about changing to remote working. Some employees work better when they are with people in an office. Others like the **structure** a working day gives them. Many do not live in a home where it is easy to work, and some worry that **colleagues** might think less of them when they see where they live.

The history of office work

Offices – places where employees **processed** the documents you need when managing a country – have been around for a long time. The Medici family's Palazzo Uffizi in Florence, or the Bank of England, are early examples. The idea of working together in one place started with factories in 18th-century Europe. Before that, city people worked in the city, country people worked in or near their homes. When factories opened, many people moved to cities to work. People are still doing this today.

In 2018, 13% of people living in cities were in thirty-three huge megacities – cities with more than 10,000,000 people. By 2030, there will probably be 14% of people living in forty-one megacities.[5]

Technology like the telephone made it possible to open offices away from the home or factory, because managers could still control things. Other new technologies like lights, and machines to do difficult maths, allowed lots of information to be saved and processed faster and in a more **organized** way than before. More employees were needed with the ability to work in these new offices. In the end, whole cities were built around business areas.

However, this brought new problems and one of the biggest was traffic. According to the RingCentral blog, any worker around the world loses about a month of each year travelling to and from work. This makes us stressed, and owning and managing a car costs money and is bad for the environment. It did not take long for people to start questioning how we work and trying to find better ways of doing it.

In the last thirty years, as offices have become bigger and more open, productivity[6] has fallen, mostly because they are so noisy, making it difficult to concentrate. People have started using **instant** messaging communication **tools**, like Slack, Teams or Skype, instead of having conversations. We probably send messages just as often as we walk over to a colleague's desk now.

The office is still a place where we can meet, discuss and share things. But we are all so busy with our own work that finding time and a place to meet is difficult. Company offices are often on different floors, buildings or even in different countries. Being close does not necessarily mean always working well together as a team.

So do we really need to be in an office? If offices are not working, is this our chance to rethink how we work? Remote working, either fully remote or mixing office and remote working, has become possible because of technology like video calls, **cloud applications** and fast internet. This means that employers can hire people from anywhere they choose, and employees can have more control over where and how they want to work. There are problems with remote working, as it is different from office work. However, once you understand what you need to do, you can work towards it.

CHAPTER ONE
Working in a remote team

Whether you are part of a team in a big company, or someone brought in from outside for a short **project**, getting to know your team is very important to your success. Here, we will look at some different types of remote workers. They can work in different businesses, and can be any age.

WFH

Working From Home (WFH) is often used in the business world. Companies give employees one day a week when they can work from home, or anywhere they choose. This saves travel time and gives workers the chance to get away for the weekend. Many businesses use this **system** because then they can have more employees than they have desks. People have started to build the WFH system into their lives, maybe working from home on Tuesdays to pick up children from school, or to go to the doctor's. In a 2019 survey, 62% of companies around the world reported that they had a flexible working system in place.[7] WFH is now a part of normal company life, the only thing that changes is the number of days in the office.

Because of the high cost of living in cities, some people live where they can afford to and travel to work for the week. These are the people you see on the early trains on Monday morning with their **laptops** and a large weekend bag. They get to work later than other people, but will work longer that evening. They either have a small apartment near work, or share a house with others, sometimes finding these online. They stay until Wednesday or Thursday night and then catch the train home and work from home for the rest of the week. People who work in other countries for three or four days a week even travel by air instead of by train.

Digital nomads

Digital nomads work for **organizations**, but choose to live in, and work from, different places. For example, Kate, who works for a **design** company in London, lives in a house in the south of Spain in summer and in the Swiss mountains during winter. Digital nomads want to travel the world and live in beautiful places that they can afford, while doing a job they enjoy. There are websites, like Nomad List or Nomadific, and there are Facebook pages that tell the nomads the best **co-working** places and the events happening there. There are difficult questions for digital nomads, like the laws for working in different countries, where to pay taxes and what documents they need. Is it really possible to relax in Goa in winter while working for a business in Amsterdam, through an Estonian company? This is still quite a new idea, so it is unclear what digital nomads and the companies employing them can or must do.

The high cost of renting homes in cities also affects people's life plans. There are places like the beaches of Bali, where you might want to live, or empty towns in Sicily, with houses being sold for €1.[8]

Hommies

Hommies, unlike the nomads, are strongly **connected** to a place. While the hommie could move to a big city or to an area where there are lots of businesses, they stay home to be close to family or just because they want to.

Hommies can be positive for country life or life in smaller towns, which have lost a lot of young people who have moved to cities to find work. Hommies do not like to travel for meetings or other company events, as they have a strong **connection** to their home town. Hommies choose to work remotely.

Gig workers

Gig workers are workers who are not employed full-time. They are **specialists** who find work online. The work can be paid "by the hour" or by project. For companies, it can be great to have a group of people to choose from who they know can do a good job. However, gig workers are not always free to work for you, as they work for many different companies.

Working towards a goal

When you know how each person in your team likes to work, it is important to be sure that everyone fully understands and works together towards one goal.

The company vision describes the company and what it is trying to achieve. This can be something big, but it must be clear. For example, Facebook wants you to: "Connect with friends and the world around you on Facebook."[9]

The mission statement is more about what the organization does. For example, Clif Bar's mission statement is easy to understand and follow: "We're working to run a different kind of company: The kind of place we'd want to work, that makes the kind of food we'd like to eat, and that tries hard for a healthier . . . world – the kind of world we'd like to pass on to our children."[10]

It is a good idea to have a company document, with goals, **values**, systems and **processes**, for everyone to see, and to share it with new employees.

Cultural differences

Remote teams are often in different countries, so you need to think carefully about **cultural** differences. In some **cultures**, people do not usually question their leaders. In other cultures where communication is more direct, people do question leaders, and the questioning may seem rude to those workers who are not used to it. Changes to the ways people work together should be made slowly, using helpful **feedback**.

Many people want to work in organizations with employees from different cultures, as it brings useful new ways of looking at projects. In a survey, 67% said that working with people from different cultures is important when they are thinking of taking a job.[11] There should, however, be **rules** so that everyone is treated with **respect**.

Who is who?

When a company has cultural rules, shared values and goals, the next step is to understand "who does what". The best companies have strong communication between employers and employees. This comes from having a clear **organizational** structure.

When a position is **created** and filled, it must be clear what the new employee has to do. This needs to be looked at again from time to time, as all positions change as a company develops. It should be clear who the person reports to and what that person is **responsible** for, so that the position works well with the rest of the organization.

Remote teams can have more flexible **responsibilities** than other teams. One person could be responsible for the team for one project and then, for another project, the team could be managed by a different person. This can work well, as people like having different responsibilities, but you need to plan and **communicate** these carefully.

Next, it is important for everyone in the remote team to be clear about who reports to whom. The easiest way to do this is to put some information about the whole team online. Describe what each person does, specialist areas, and even a few words about successes. Not everybody is comfortable writing about themselves, so it is better to choose one person as a "journalist" for the whole team, or bring in a specialist to do this.

Team size

Katherine Klein at the University of Pennsylvania developed the idea that six is the magic number for a team.[12] Although teams between four and nine are good, six is particularly good for remote teams who meet on video calls. There is a fall in productivity connected to team size known as the "Ringelmann effect".[13] In a competition between two teams, Ringelmann discovered that adding more people to the team did not increase the ability of the team because some people did not work. Jeff Bezos, of Amazon, thinks that the best team size is the one that only needs two pizzas for dinner.[14] He believes that larger teams do not work as well because it takes more work to manage them.

The team size of six remote workers can work well without a leader if the structure of communication and meetings is well organized. But smaller teams can cost more for a business because you need more team leader positions, and they are paid more. In a team of six, there will be people with more and less experience. This is healthy, as less experienced people learn, while more experienced people have to **organize** their own thoughts to explain things.

The system does not stop here, as you can have six of these teams managed by one person, and six of these leaders of teams of six managed by one person. In remote teams, this system helps keep things together and gets everybody communicating.

Collective knowledge

Collective knowledge is the information that an organization holds about itself. This is not only about how things work, but processes, quick ways of doing things, and information about specialists and where to find them. Building the collective knowledge in a remote team means checking that the information is saved and easily shared with the team.

A good way of doing this is by having a shared drive, somewhere where you record all meetings, talks, presentations, as well as notes, files and **research** papers. Online or cloud whiteboards can be used to collect or share ideas. And all the company's **marketing branding** can be kept on a separate computer drive.

One person in the company should be responsible for creating this collective knowledge system and sharing it with teams.

CHAPTER TWO
Communicating in a remote team

Rules of communication

Communication is the most important part of creating a successful remote team. Without the little signs you get from face-to-face communication, remote workers have to **improve** at communicating **virtually**. This can be learned.

Teams need to decide and agree on communication systems, which everybody can use. This is very important for new employees. The whole team must know how to use the right technology to communicate their messages. There is a place for email, instant messaging, video calls and other types of communication. Each team will have a way of communicating that works for it.

Here is an example from Basecamp, a remote computer program company:

- "Speaking only helps the people in the room, writing helps everyone."
- "Five people in a room for an hour isn't a one-hour meeting, it's a five-hour meeting."
- "Poor communication creates more work."

Direct ways of communicating

Finding the most direct way for a manager to communicate well with the person doing a **task** is very important in remote working. With lots of people working on a project, this can be difficult. People may live in different **time zones**, or not understand how important something is.

In the workplace, it is much easier to get quick answers as you can see if someone is free or busy. In remote work, where you cannot see the team, this becomes more difficult. When using **chat** applications, people often want to send messages to lots of people just to get a quick answer. However, this slows everything down as people cannot concentrate on their work. To be sure that answers are managed well:

- Send a quick message to say you have seen a question and that you will reply as soon as you can.
- Keep your **calendar** up to date so that people know when you are free to answer their questions.
- Create a virtual "office hour" in your calendar every week when employees can ask you questions.

Good and bad video calls

In the post-coronavirus world, the video call is king. A bad call is: two hours, with twenty people, and a poor internet connection. But what makes a great video call?

- Have a good camera and **microphone**.
- Only invite the people who need to be there; share information with other people later if necessary.

- There is no reason why a video call cannot be only fifteen minutes long.
- Follow the meeting **agenda**. Check that everyone has the agenda and any documents needed before the call.
- Choose someone who is responsible for following the agenda and planning future meetings if necessary.
- It can be useful to have a different person responsible for timekeeping.
- Somebody should also take **minutes**, to record any actions to be taken after the meeting.

Synchronous and asynchronous communication

According to the *Harvard Business Review*'s "**Collaborative** Overload", the time employees spend on **collaboration** has increased by 50% in the past twenty years.[15] Workers often spend 80% of their workdays communicating with colleagues by email (about six hours a day); in meetings (about 15% of a company's time); and using instant messaging **apps** (Slack users send about 250 messages a day[16]).

So how should you manage all the messages received? Teams could agree to answer messages in twenty-four hours. You can have a group on a messaging app, like WhatsApp, for emergencies. Most of the instant messaging **services** have something called a snooze **setting** that helps you remember that messages are waiting.

All these things are examples of synchronous communication, when lots of people are communicating at the same time, in a meeting room or in a face-to-face conversation. Answers are given or actions taken immediately.

This type of communication creates a culture of "always on" in an organization, even when this is not necessary. It also means that workers have little time to concentrate on actually doing their work.

Asynchronous communication is different. It is where an answer is not immediate, but can happen after some time.

It is important to get the right balance of synchronous and asynchronous communication.

The Eisenhower **Decision** Principle can help you organize your day and concentrate. By following its rules, a team can agree on a system to decide the kind of message or task it is looking at.

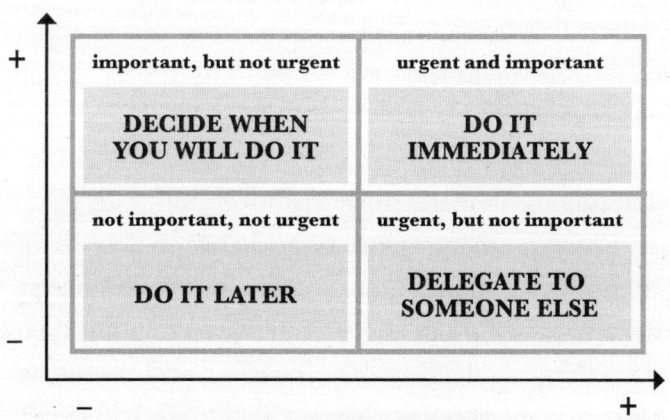

Figure 1: Eisenhower Decision Principle

When the team fully understands what is urgent and what is important, people will not feel the **stress** of having to reply to everything immediately. They will not reply unless something is both important and urgent.

Asynchronous communication works best with longer pieces of "deep work"[17], when you need to be able to concentrate on a difficult task. Deep work is what allows a company to work well and every company needs to create the right environment to let this happen. Deep work cannot happen in an environment where synchronous communication is strong.

"Flow state" is when you are fully concentrated on an activity. Flow state in the workplace leads to developing real understanding or ability. This is because a person thinks and collects information, and they are motivated to work harder because they need to learn if they are to achieve better results. Flow state is usually used in **creative** and technical work that requires a lot of **concentration**.[18]

The right communication for the task

However, deep work, flow state and asynchronous communication alone do not make a company immediately more productive. You need to find the right balance in making deep work possible, but without totally stopping synchronous communication. Not all teams need as much time for deep work.

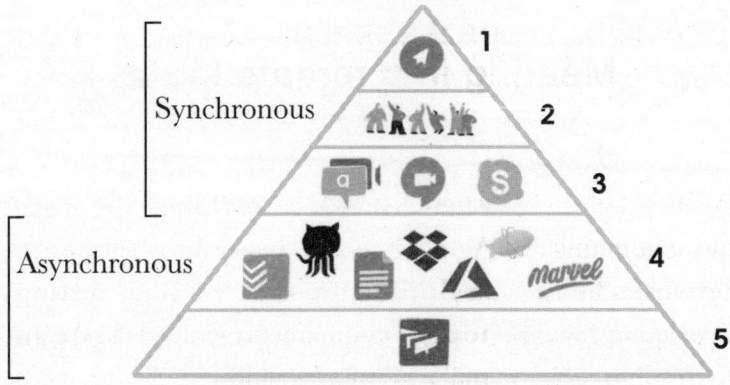

1. In emergencies
2. Going away or meeting up as a whole company or in smaller teams
3. Monthly 1:1s, team meetings, or meetings when needed to discuss very difficult topics
4. Giving feedback on documents, design or tasks, etc.
5. A virtual centre for news, ideas, feedback, having fun and everything in between

Figure 2: Synchronous and asynchronous communication[19] shows when to use which type of communication.

Asynchronous communication improves productivity by making deep work easier. Because things are written and shared with everyone, it creates a system for discussing and making decisions. It is also important when bringing new people into a team because they can see the conversations that have already happened.

CHAPTER THREE
Meeting in a remote team

The workplace is where we meet, **collaborate**, create and communicate. We do not only have new ideas, create **networks** and build **relationships** in the formal **settings** of meetings, **workshops** or company presentations. We also do this through informal meetings in a lift, over coffee, eating lunch together, or at after-work events. These meetings get us noticed in the company and can develop our careers. It is also how we learn about what everyone else is doing, usually just by **chatting**!

When you work remotely, this is not as easy, but you can do it.

Virtual coffee breaks and lunches

You can create a virtual coffee **break channel** with your favourite messaging app, and when someone wants a ten-minute break, they get a coffee and post the message "coffee time" or a video **link**. Anyone who is around and feels like a break can join.

If unplanned coffee breaks are not working, then you can plan a time, maybe once in the morning and once in the afternoon, when everyone who is free can stop for a chat.

In the office, there are often lunchtime meetings with food, with a speaker and informal questions and answers. You can do this online, **delivering** lunch to people before the meeting.

Organizing events

Since the pandemic lockdowns, there have been a lot of online events, like food-, wine- or beer-tastings where people ordered online and got together on a video call for a tasting **session**.

Some sports activities are also possible using group apps, like Strava, where people share what they achieve for activities like running or cycling.

A good way to bring teams together is to have a quiz night, when you simply ask questions from the internet and score yourself, or use Zoom and then send your answers to the organizer on the messaging app. Working in teams and creating healthy competition between teams can bring people together. You could try programs like Mentimeter or Kahoot!, which have tools for questions and immediate results.

You could also have meetings where women in the company can discuss the problems they have in their careers and share useful ideas and information.

In-person meetings, short breaks and away days

It is good for working relationships to bring teams together from time to time. While it is possible to work for years with someone and only have contact by video calls, it is always much better to meet in person – in the same place. It is good for new starters to meet the other people in the team and create the kind of relationships that will make good communication possible. Remotehub.io, the remote hiring website, notes 106 remote companies that organize breaks once a year for their teams.[20]

Sharing an agenda for a break and carefully following it can seem formal, but everybody needs to understand the goals if it is to be successful. The experience of a well-organized event achieving all its goals gives the event more value. A badly planned and organized event will stop people wanting to be part of other events in the future.

As with any business away day, the agenda could mix workshops, sessions to share ideas about the direction of the company, as well as some training, **coaching** or team-building activities.

A training day or a workshop is a great way to bring a remote team together to share a learning experience. It also gives people the chance to get to know each other informally during the breaks, at lunch or after the event has ended.

Idea-sharing sessions can bring people together from different teams, if they do not usually work together. They help find answers to problems, and can also help to build better relationships across the company.

Another type of team-building event creates experiences shared on special days. This could be going to a beautiful or important place, or listening to a well-known person talking. Informal settings give remote teams the chance to build relationships and start conversations.

With a little **creativity**, we can build stronger **social** relationships with our colleagues, customers, and other people we work with.

Places to work

There used to be places where people went to work, while sometimes they worked from home. With remote working, we can now choose between working from home, co-working, and even **co-living**. It is important to understand that a co-working **space** is different from a café with a free internet connection. Co-working spaces give us the right place and **equipment** for work, and they also give us a chance to mix and develop relationships with people. They are also places where you can concentrate better than at home.

Co-working spaces as communities

Just as it is important to make a **community** out of a remote team, it is also important for people to be part of the communities that they live in. This helps to stop people feeling alone.

Getting ready in the morning, then walking or cycling to a co-working centre can be positive for a remote worker. Firstly, it is a break between home and the workplace, and this creates limits around the working day. We can all imagine a remote worker wearing informal clothes in a small home office with no windows, and not going out for days. Secondly, walking or cycling will get you moving and ready for a day at the co-working space.

Co-working spaces create communities, because you meet near the coffee machine and start conversations, or go to events that are organized by the co-working centre.

This can bring new ways of looking at things that can help you in your work. If other people in the co-working centre do the same type of work, it might be possible to collaborate or share problems.

There are many co-working spaces in towns and cities, and it is worth doing some research as you will find different types of people in each one. For example, there may be **designers** in one co-working space, while computer engineers will prefer another. Some co-working spaces **market** themselves to one special group.

You can also hire private "smart offices" for small teams or companies. Just like co-working centres, these will have meeting rooms and collaboration spaces as well as the normal offices or workspaces. The big difference is that the remote worker in a co-working centre will have links with colleagues in lots of different places, and also everyday contact with people outside their work setting, or non-work colleagues.

Co-living and co-working

Co-living and co-working can go together, giving the digital nomad a great chance to meet, live with and work with other digital nomads. More and more, co-living spaces are also being used as places for company breaks. These spaces already have somewhere for people to stay and work, and you can **research** and find them easily online.

The most important thing about co-living is the chance it gives you to join a community easily. Co-working is already in place for community, and co-living goes even further.

Co-living works best for a short time. Although it can be great for meeting people who think like you, it might lead you to live only with digital nomads and not people from the wider community, **limiting** how you see life.

New technologies and data security

Many cheaper, new technologies like fast internet, cloud computing, personal laptops, mobile phones and video calls, have made it possible to move work away from the office, so we can choose where, when and how we work.

Remote teams need three things: data security, the right equipment and the technology in the workplace needed to work remotely.

Data security is often used as a reason for not working remotely, and it should be taken seriously. An employee's data security is as much in danger working at home as in an office. The tools and training needed to keep data safe are the same in both situations. Either you or your security officer need to check that everybody on the team knows how to look after themselves and report problems.

It is a good idea to give the remote worker a laptop that is only used for work. If a remote worker uses their own equipment, then as a company you have no idea if or how well the data is being kept safe.

Office organization and equipment

For good remote working you need to mix technology and services. You will need:

- A fast internet connection.
- A good camera, microphone and headphones.
- A **screen** and keyboard, not just a laptop.
- A video-calling service, not a free one like Skype or Hangouts, or the time- or number-limited group calls on Zoom or whereby.com. The paid services, on Zoom, Microsoft Teams or G Suite Hangouts, are better for remote team business calls.
- Messaging apps. Important for asynchronous communication. It is helpful to have someone responsible for the groups because they can quickly become confusing.
- Cloud space. Documents must be kept on a system that everyone on the team can enter and use quickly.
- Remote whiteboards. Cloud-**based** whiteboards are good for remote teams. They allow them to collaborate online using virtual tools, asynchronously.
- An **automated** place to manage remote teams' spending on company credit cards, or to pay people back for money they have spent while working.

CHAPTER FOUR
Managing a remote team

Office-based or remote

What makes a good remote manager? As you would do in the office, you will need to get the best work from your team; you will **set** goals, organize **progress** reports, help manage problems and report what the team achieves. In a remote setting, you can work in different ways and try new things that you could not do in the office. For example, you can look at how the team achieves goals instead of how long people spend at their desks. You can concentrate on the important things, instead of listening to the people who shout the loudest. As a remote manager, you will develop the ability to set and manage goals and get results, which will really make your team work better.

Office-based manager	Remote manager
9–5 hours: your team will all probably work at the same times. You will see them at their desks or in meetings.	**Flexibility**: your team can work when it is best for them. You will need to allow them to organize their time.
Being present: an employee's value may be **assessed** against how much they can be seen in the office.	**Goal-based assessment**: remote working allows managers to look at results instead of hours worked.

Hierarchical structure: the office usually has a chain of managers who decide things.	**Flat structure**: each employee should be responsible for their own work and how they decide to do it.
Face-to-face communication: employees may be motivated by being thanked in front of colleagues for good work.	**Remote communication**: make time to notice good work and bring it to the attention of the rest of the team.
Being seen: your employees will probably work near you and can ask for help at any time.	**Virtual reality**: put conversations with your team in your calendar often, and keep it up to date so they know when you are free.

Collaboration and communication: the five conversations

According to Gallup workplace research, managers should have conversations with their remote teams often.[21] These conversations can be formal or more informal. The manager should try to motivate the team to be innovative. This will help them do well, and feel a part of the team and not alone.

The Gallup research **listed** five types of manager–employee conversations:
- quick connection
- check-in to see how they are doing
- career coaching
- progress **assessment**
- developing the job and relationships.

These five types of conversation drive how well the team does. To achieve results, you must have these different types of conversations often and manage questions in the right way: direct questions get direct answers. The goal of these conversations for employees is to keep them feeling part of a team. For managers, it helps them to understand remote employees by thinking about what each one brings to the team, seeing how they communicate and noticing how they manage workplace situations.

What did you work on today?

A very helpful exercise used by the company Basecamp is an automated question at the end of every workday: "What did you work on today?"[22]. Answers are shared with everyone in the company, shown on one page and listed by date, so everybody can see what is going on in the company. Basecamp see this as a good exercise for teams to think about their work and understand everyone's responsibilities. They also use the same system weekly and add some informal questions, which employees do not have to answer, like "What book are you reading?" or "What are you doing this weekend?".

Your communication tools

There are several important communication tools for remote teams. The chat applications, Slack, Teams, Hangouts or Discord, mostly do the same things. You can use them to create groups that are private or not, and you can make video calls or direct message people. The most important thing to do when creating groups is to give them clear names so that the whole company is not chatting all day long in one group, making it impossible to follow who is talking about what and to whom. It is also good to get people to chat in groups rather than direct messages, so that information is shared. If possible, connect the video-calling application so it is easy to call someone rather than write long messages.

The use of **emojis** is not easy, as people of different ages do not always know what they mean. It could be helpful to list the main ones to use. Emojis allow people to show something about themselves and can be positive for the team. They can also be used to mark a post as useful (but agree which emoji to use). If nothing more, a 👍 shows that you have read something.

Hybrid teams

Today, there are a lot more **hybrid** teams, with office-based workers and remote workers, as companies move to manage **social distancing** and flexible working.

A hybrid team can be one of the most difficult things about managing a remote team. You need to create systems that allow all employees to work together. Talk to your team about how you can best do this. Discuss when and how you will communicate, and agree that all team meetings will be online, as hybrid meetings are unfair to those who are not in the office. Set some rules for meetings: questions to be asked in the chat channels, read out by the person responsible for the meeting, with enough time for everyone to answer.

It is hard to notice when people have good or bad relationships when some are in the office and some are remote. It is very easy for a workplace group to have lunch together or go out after work and forget about remote colleagues. You cannot stop this, but there should be minutes of what is discussed, shared and decided at meetings, so everyone knows what is happening.

One good way of connecting teams is to have a friend system, putting one remote person with an office-based person. This means that the remote person knows what is happening at the office, and there is also someone they can message quickly, for example, to find out if someone in the office is at their desk.

Check that the office people use the chat channels where possible. If teams discuss things in person, someone should write notes of the conversation, and the actions and dates decided. These notes should be put in a shared document that everyone can see.

One problem for hybrid teams is that people can concentrate better in a remote environment than in the office. This is very important if there are people on the team who spend most of their time in the workplace, as it will change the amount of deep work they do. Explain that it would be better if they did the deep work when working remotely, or save a space in the calendar to concentrate on deep work without being interrupted.

Creating a virtual safe space

Just like in real life, creating virtual safe spaces is important for the wellbeing of all employees. Virtual meetings can be difficult because you cannot see people's faces or other social signs as well as you can during in-person meetings.

Setting some rules will make all work events, from chat channels to meetings, safe spaces for all:

1. Check everybody is part of social chat: some people might not feel able to talk about some topics. For example, discussing expensive holidays or restaurants might make some colleagues feel uncomfortable.
2. Check chat spaces for language that leaves some employees out.
3. Create a word that can be used to show people that they are talking or acting in an incorrect way during meetings.
4. Everyone in the team should feel free to say what they think.

It is also important that the team understands these things:

- Good communication is very important: creating a safe space will make everyone feel **valued** and **respected** and able to do their best work.

- If someone asks a question in private, share the answer, as other people might have the same question.
- Tell everyone when tasks or other important things have been achieved.
- Invite employees to use open channels to share questions, answers, successes, news and things that they are worried about.
- Remember to send company news by email, not every day, but more often than every month, so teams do not feel forgotten.
- Spend time and money on **project management** tools, so teams can see what they are doing and how it helps other people's work in the company. But check that everybody is comfortable using the tools.

CHAPTER FIVE
Managing goals and performance

Managing by results

For a team to work well, everybody has to concentrate on real results, not on the process of achieving them. Employees then have a lot of independence, using their own abilities to reach goals in their own way. The opposite way of managing, which is often called command and control, means managers check everything that their employees are doing. There are lots of reasons why you should not manage in this way, but it is impossible in a remote setting. Instead, by concentrating on results, you can allow your team to be free to control their time, while it also makes it easier for them to take responsibility for achieving their goals.

Unlike in an office setting, where you can put up a big **dashboard** with the important information and results for everyone to see, it is difficult to show and share a team's results in a remote setting. The best way to share this information is to check that all employees can see it on the communication channels and to motivate people to look at online dashboards with messages like "almost there on this month's goals" and "10 days to go before month-end" with a link. There are dashboards for all sorts of different company information, like weekdone.com or Hubspot.

To use a results-driven way of working:
- Communicate the company's goals to get everyone moving in the same direction, build good relationships, and make anyone on the team who might feel lost part of the team.
- Motivate all employees to achieve a lot and feel responsible for the work they do.
- Make communication more open so that everyone feels that they are collaborating as part of a team.
- Set goals to push people to achieve, succeed and continue learning. Collect feedback and use it to improve processes and organizational culture.

Goal setting

An **aligned** team is one that is trying to achieve the same thing, understands its goals and has people who know how to use their abilities for the good of the team. Team **alignment** becomes even more important when you work remotely or as a hybrid. As a manager, how do you know that each person is aligned and understands what success is for their team?

- Look at past goals when choosing new goals: were the goals good enough? What was done well? What was learned from any problems?
- It must be possible to **measure** results in numbers; check that the team can achieve them without working too hard.

- Make your team own and be responsible for their work.
- Discuss the new goals in video calls, first with each person and then in a team meeting – you must communicate what you want so that it is clear to all.
- Check and share progress towards the goal; break the goal into different steps to be achieved.
- Learn about each person's abilities and how they are improving, so that you can help them achieve their best work.

Accountability

Accountability is the responsibility of each person to complete the task they have been given. To make this work in a remote setting, there must be clear reporting structures, goals and meetings (video calls and screen sharing for close collaboration). The most important thing is that there is a person **accountable** for each task or project. If you want a remote team to work at its best, people must trust each other, and accountability helps with this. ReCharge, the remote-first company with over 250 employees working in different time zones, asks people to tick the projects they are accountable for on a task **list**.[23] These task lists are linked to a time. Without this, there would be no responsibility for completing them on time.

Constructive accountability

Managers can use constructive accountability to develop the abilities of the team by moving accountability into everyday work. According to J. G. Seiling, constructive accountability is a conversation that creates a working relationship while doing the work, and creates group responsibility for each result.[24] For this to work, it is important for managers to think carefully about who should be in team sessions, and at times they should let the team manage itself. Managers should ask their teams to discuss and share their ideas on what could be done better. This leads to collaborative accountability and means that the team continues to work together better.

Ownership

There must be someone who explains what has to be decided (decision-maker) and someone who will drive the research and decision process (**owner**). You need to check that everybody working with the team, inside or outside the company, knows who the decision-maker and owner are. If projects are collaborative, each part of the project must have an owner responsible for the work and for correct information.

Ownership motivates the people in a team to think and find ways forward. Managers should not be giving all the answers and directions because this stops people from being **independent**. This is not good in remote teams as the goal is to limit the need for communication. The idea of "extreme ownership" can be used in a remote working system. Every person in the team has to "own" one area of the business or project. For new people on the team, taking ownership does not mean they are on their own from the first day. They will need help and time to learn the process. The culture of ownership leads to better and faster decision-making.

Measuring performance and tracking progress

Managing **performance** plans well can bring down costs, increase productivity and give teams a well-balanced and healthy environment to work in. Managers should always measure performance in the same way and, most importantly, give feedback about it to their teams. The way you measure performance changes a little when teams are remote, and it is very important to create the tools early so that the culture of the company is open. In remote working, you cannot always see how someone is managing. In an office, this is a little easier, although it can sometimes be difficult to tell the difference between busy and productive, even when you are sitting next to someone.

Objectives and Key Results (OKRs) and Key Performance Indicators (KPIs)

You can measure performance in numbers by using a system called **Objectives** and **Key** Results (OKRs) and having a clear link between business needs and goals, which in turn give you the **Key Performance Indicators** (KPIs). Start by introducing the team's objectives and then divide the team goals into goals for each person. The results must be discussed often, and the business goals may need to change sometimes with changes in the market.

The team must be able to change direction quickly if necessary, as this, and the ability to continue towards a goal, are important to the success of a team.

Kaizen or Continuous Improvement (CI)

Kaizen or Continuous **Improvement** (CI) was introduced in Japan after the Second World War to help rebuild Japanese companies. CI is about trying to make things as good as they can be, by making small changes all the time. One of the important things about CI is to measure and look at what has led to a problem, using the "Five Why" system (you keep asking why until you get the answer to your problem).

Performance management tools

There are many new performance management tools. Some are automated or have a cost; others need planning, time and work before they can be used by your teams.

You must introduce any tool that you use to the whole team by explaining what it does and what it should achieve. The results collected must be discussed among the managers, and positive change must come out of it. Many companies start with the right idea, but fail to make positive use of the information.

As you would in the office setting, try to give feedback in a positive way, discussing what went wrong and what can be learned from the experience. It may be necessary to record several actions, and check that people do them. When there are problems, make notes about them and the actions agreed. Check that everybody knows their responsibilities and plan future meetings. This shows that you want the team to learn from the problem and that it will not end with no action taken.

It is very important to get employees to trust you in remote settings, because it is easy to misunderstand each other. You can do this by showing respect for your employees in your actions. For example:
- Do not cancel meetings with your employees at the last minute.
- Do not instantly agree with the customer or a manager instead of your team.
- Try to be fair to the whole team.

CHAPTER SIX
Decision-making, mediation and progression

Every time you succeed or fail, every chance taken or missed is the result of a decision that was made or not made by someone. Businesses are managed by decisions, and in many companies the decision-making process often stops progress.

High-**performing** teams make the right decision quickly and can be trusted to take action. In a remote environment, it can be very difficult to get everyone together in a meeting to discuss a decision. You cannot always get face-to-face communication. So you need a process based on the same idea as asynchronous communication.

Asynchronous decision-making

Asynchronous decision-making is a great way for your team to move forward and take decisions without a lot of meetings. It is used a lot in open source projects. Open source means anybody is free to use, change and share a project, so it is easier to collaborate and make better decisions.[25] It is amazing to see how people come together and collaborate on a project that has an end goal, without meeting, simply through asynchronous communication. This type of decision-making needs a lot of planning and begins by creating a process, which has a communication channel at the centre with a strong system to help people to work together. The best way to do this is to have one channel to discuss ideas and another for people to decide which idea they want to choose.

In remote settings, getting everybody to agree can slow progress, so if you cannot get everyone to agree it is better if most people do. There are lots of different programs which you can buy today that help with this type of decision-making process. They can be used with any communication and project management tool in a company.

You could do this:
- Give people the job of making a decision.
- Start discussing it online.
- Write some plans and ask people to choose the best one.
- Share the results and actions to be taken.

If you use asynchronous decision-making, productivity will increase because you are motivating collaboration and making better use of time. When a decision has been made, a plan has to be put into action by choosing an owner who is responsible for delivering the results, who can take any problems to the decision-maker and let everybody know what is happening.

Conflict resolution and mediation

There can be **conflict** in remote teams just as there can be in any working environment. You cannot, nor should not, try to stay away from it. It can often be a way to move forward. Arguing over difficult problems is an important part of how a company works. In a remote work setting, teams should build good ways of doing this into their work.

The best way is to develop a process for managing conflict that is part of the company culture and known by everybody. If it is part of normal day-to-day business, it will not seem so difficult to manage. And it will stop conflict from becoming bigger and hurting people. If a worker feels able to ask for **mediation** to find a **resolution** to a conflict, it is a sign of a healthy company culture. Managing conflict in remote work can be easier than face-to-face since it becomes a recorded process, and the process becomes part of company culture.

Mediators, usually managers or team leaders, are important, and they need to have training. For mediation to be successful, people must trust and respect the mediator, and there should be good channels of communication to find quick resolutions for problems.

Arguing in writing

People often argue in writing in the chat channels, not in formal documents. Because online chat is instant, people do not always think before they answer, and it is easy to read things incorrectly. And, while it is good that there is a record of what was "said" and when, you can still miss things. You can check information if you are communicating in person, but in written communication you cannot always understand the situation or how a person feels. According to Allan and Barbara Pease writing in the *New York Times*, more than 50% of communication is not done in words.[26] This shows some of the problems you could have with chat channels.

Arguing in person

Although you do not record anything when you are arguing in person, it is still very real. But, as the manager, you can only know what each person says happened. Arguing in person is rare in the remote working setting, as a lot of the communication is done using chat or email.

Mediation

The first step for anyone who finds themselves in a conflict situation is to ask for mediation from their manager or team leader. Sometimes, it may be a team leader who asks for mediation and asks their manager for help.

The goal of mediation is to have a clear understanding of the conflict and take away any strong feelings from the discussion. Here are the steps in the mediation process:

- The mediator speaks to everybody in the conflict and writes the points of the conflict that are important to each side. This must be recorded.
- The mediator sends these written points from the conversations to each person to check.
- If people have been arguing in writing, the mediator collects the documents recording the conversations and makes a list of the important points.
- All sides are invited to a video call, if all are remote, to find a resolution to the conflict. The agenda is carefully planned before the meeting and is based on the mediator saying what the important points of the conversations are. Then each person can talk.

The mediator then works with everybody to find an answer to the problem where possible.
- The result of the meeting is sent out in writing.

The mediator does the important job of finding a way for everyone to meet in the middle and be able to move on. The goal is to stop people arguing. How is this done? There is more than one way, but the mediator should work with everybody to:
- understand each person's way of thinking
- change their **behaviour**
- look at what they have agreed from time to time
- share work more fairly and give greater responsibility.

Feeling happy at work

Feeling happy at work means that you like your job. You know what you are doing, what you have achieved and what you can do. You feel that your team and other people in your business respect you. Remote working is no different. But remote workers may have different ideas about what makes them like their jobs.

Most people enjoy doing things to the best of their ability, and being given the responsibility to make decisions and be part of something. The difference between an office-based worker and a remote worker is that the office worker usually works "normal working" hours, while a remote worker may enjoy being flexible, being able to look after children, take a longer lunch break and spend time in the sun. But the reasons for

motivation are not important. What is important is that companies with happy employees perform 20% better than the competition.

Here are some steps you can take to create a happy, productive team:

- Say "well done" often; this is best in front of other people in the team.
- Hold a weekly ten-minute Zoom call to talk about any successes.
- Create a Slack channel where team members can share news that they are proud of.
- Write an instant note when you notice someone doing more than they have to. This can really motivate your team.

Make work matter. No one wants to feel that their work does not matter. Check that each employee knows why they are doing what they are doing and how important it is. Zappos are a good example. They deliver shoes and clothes, but their mission is to "deliver happiness". All new employees spend two weeks taking customer service calls, no matter what job they are going to be doing, so they see the value of their work.

Spend time thinking about how your team can develop as people and workers. When employees feel they are not developing, that is when they start looking for something new. People feel happy when they are growing and increasing their abilities.

You could:
- Pay towards online or in-person classes, courses or meetings for employees who want to learn something new.
- Have "lunch and learns", where someone from inside or outside the team talks about something they love.
- Start a book or film club.

Career progression

Remote workers have goals and dreams, too. They should have the same type of career development systems as office-based workers. Career progression is the process used by managers to allow their teams to plan different ways of developing their careers based on what abilities they need for a position.

Career progression is important if you want to keep your team. Managers should motivate their employees to develop their abilities and maybe find a way to become specialists in an area. This could be by paying for training, getting them to research and write about it, or speak at events.

Managers need to discuss what their employees' goals and dreams are and **track** their progress. It is important to talk about these often and use a whole video call to do it. Or, as well as the four-monthly team meetings, take time for each person on the team. One-on-one meetings are a great place for these discussions. Record the conversations, by making a note of the action points, and check back at the next session to see what progress has been made or any changes that are needed.

Develop career path planning for your team or company:
- Ask the team about success: what is a win?
- Continue to repeat the organization's goal and what part they have in it.
- Create short-and-long-term goals, and a process for career progression.
- Talk to the team often and keep the goals at the front of everybody's mind.
- Track performance and measure results using performance management tools.
- Communicate results, and give feedback often.
- Help teams to make decisions and to take action.
- Most importantly, say "well done" in front of the team when people succeed; discuss things one-to-one when they do not.

CHAPTER SEVEN
Hiring employees

Finding the best people for the job is one of the hardest things for companies to do. Allowing people to work remotely can help with this. A survey by Owl Labs reported that remote companies in the US take 33% less time to hire employees, and companies that help people work remotely have 25% lower employee turnover (people leaving) than those that do not.[27]

So how can companies use this to build a winning team?

Employer branding

To hire the top people, a company must spend money on their online branding. It is the first thing the future employee sees about the hiring company. So it should show the friendly culture and what working remotely for the company looks like.

People join a company because:
- they love what it does and want to be part of the process
- they love the environment and the way that the company works
- they see that the company cares for the wellbeing of its employees.

Future employees will ask present and past employees in their network for advice or ideas, so:

- Companies should be seen in the right places, like LinkedIn, Glassdoor, Twitter, Medium. Surveys have shown that 83% of people looking for jobs research a company online before they **apply**.[28]
- List people in the team that they will work with, not just the leaders, on the website.

Interview process

How does a manager assess a person's abilities? The best way is to create a situation like the environment the person will be working in. This will test if the person will be successful. For example, if the position requires mostly written communication and lots of video calls, then it is important to get an idea of how the candidate manages using these. The **interview** process for the position would have a written part (text-based interview); and a part using video calls, with other people from the team if possible.

It is always a really good idea to have another person join the interview, so that you can hear what they think, too. If this is not possible, ask if you can record the interview for the team to watch in their own time, and be a part of the hiring process.

Remote jobs can be open to anyone, anywhere in the world. You should give information about time zones so that you do not have too many applications. Pay for the position should also be made clear.

Behaviour-based interviewing

Behavioural interviewing is a great way to understand how a person works remotely. This is important when building a remote team because the behaviour of people on the team and their relationships is even more important when they are in different places.

Ask questions like: "How do you organize your day, and how do you decide which tasks to do first?", "How would you manage not having face-to-face contact when you work remotely?" or "If you had a problem when the rest of your remote team was not online, what would you do about it?".

According to Toggl, a time-tracking app and remote-first company, the things that remote companies look for when hiring are the ability to communicate and be organized, and to work well in a team environment.[29] People must be able to work in a way that leads to their highest productivity, in any environment, using to-do lists, flow boards (a business app that helps manage tasks you repeat) and time tracking.

During an interview, Toggl also looks into things like the ability to collaborate virtually, being open, and not losing concentration when working from home. They ask questions about people's ability to look after themselves, like taking enough breaks every day and their ability to relax after work.

When you are interviewing, remember that a good remote worker:

- communicates well
- is organized and comfortable working remotely for a long time
- can make decisions and take action on their own.

Pay for remote employees

How much to pay remote employees is a difficult topic. What happens when you have two people doing the same job but living in different cities? Or when an employee moves to a cheaper city than the one that they were living in before? Creating a fair pay structure is very important if you want your team to trust you. It is a lot of work for companies if they need to keep looking at and changing the pay structures.

Pay can be **structured** in three different ways:

- A global salary model pays everyone the same. It does not matter where they are.
- A local salary model pays according to the cost of living where the person lives.
- A hybrid salary model mixes the other two models.

Onboarding

Hiring is only one step of the process when building a remote team. The next step, onboarding, or welcoming those hired and getting them ready for success, is important if you want to keep new employees.

There should be a clear onboarding system in place. Each step of the process must be agreed in documents across the company, and followed.

In an office, a new employee might be taken to lunch, and given training and a chance to meet the team informally. The same kind of thing should be done remotely, so that a new remote employee understands the company, the position and the team.

It is a good idea to create a company document to share with new employees when they start work. It should have the company's goals, values, systems and processes, and any other information that might help employees to do their work. The document should be ready as soon as teams become remote, and changed as the company grows and develops.

Although each company will have its own onboarding system, there are three important steps:
- Step 1: welcome new people to the team either by email or through the messaging apps.
- Step 2: give the new employee their first task or project. This will make them feel excited about the new position and help increase productivity. The new employee could work on a group project, which will help them build relationships with their colleagues. Or you can give them a project to do on their own, while they learn how the remote team works. Group projects are usually easier for people who already have experience of working in remote teams.
- Step 3: contact the new employee after a week or two to see how they are doing and to get feedback. If possible, the team leader should talk to the new

employee two more times during their first three months, as they may have questions or require more information on how things are done.

Offboarding

In a remote company, every step an employee takes is important. So companies must also **design** an offboarding system for when people leave. Research by a UK marketing company found that only 29% of remote organizations have a formal employee exit process. But successful offboarding systems are important to help organizations grow, and employees to stay and perform well in the company. The important steps in the process are to understand why people leave, to give responsibility for all projects to another person on the team, and to stop people being able to use company digital systems after they leave.

In an office, when people decide to leave, managers and colleagues still see them every day for a few weeks. That allows time to manage work and relationships. However, in a remote setting, time can pass quickly, and the employee could leave without doing this.

Exit interviews are the best way to understand why someone is leaving. They can be a useful tool in keeping employees in future if you look at the feedback. It can also allow you to collect information on how the culture of the company is seen by the employees, which is important in a remote environment, when the manager might not know what their team's experiences are.

You can also give the person who is leaving the chance to leave in a positive way, by thanking them for the work they have done remotely.

An offboarding process should:
- check that the process of passing a project to another person on the team is going well
- have an exit interview
- get company equipment back from the employee
- ask employees to sign any necessary documents.

CHAPTER EIGHT
Self-care

Things to do every day

When working remotely, especially from home, it can be very hard to set limits between your own time and work time. Research has found that most remote workers find it difficult to relax after work, feel alone and cannot concentrate.[30]

So, how can you get the most from remote working, while looking after yourself? Take a couple of minutes to think about the way you work:

- What is your place of work?
- Has your workstation got comfortable furniture?
- Are you planning breaks from your workstation during the day?
- How do you plan your workdays?
- How do you start your working day?
- How do you end your working day?
- Are you staying active? Eating healthily? Sleeping well?
- Are you taking time off?
- What do you do to look after yourself?
- What makes you lose concentration in your workspace, and what do you do about it?
- Are your home and workspace clean?

- Do you sometimes feel alone or very stressed?
- Are you part of a community outside your work?
- Are you planning your career development?

Your workspace

How many hours do you spend in your workspace? Six to eight at least; even longer? Checking you have the right workspace is important to productivity. It can be a desk in your home, a desk in a co-working space or shared office, or it can be a place in a café near home – even better, mix all of them.

How you achieve a productive workspace will change according to the way you work. According to Catherine Avery, owner of productivitybydesign.com, productivity happens only when one uses a space only for work. She says that if you do not have a special workspace, you show that the work you do does not matter. It is a mistake lots of people make when they work remotely.[31]

Creating your workspace should not be difficult. Choosing somewhere in a less-used room is possible, but do not have your desk in a place where you cannot concentrate or you will be uncomfortable, like a dining table or a bed. The best place is in a room with a door, so that you can be shut away and interrupted only if needed.

One of the good things about working remotely is that it gives you the chance to change your setting as often as you like. You can work three days a week in your own workspace and two days a week in a café. Or you can work a few days in your garden or at your dining table and the rest of the time in your workspace. Moving from space to space is a good way to keep your concentration and be productive, because you do not get bored.

Brie Reynolds, career development **coach** and specialist in flexible and remote jobs, thinks that changes of environment are good. In an interview in Business Insider, Brie said that "different spaces in the home lend themselves to different kinds of work".[32] No environment is good for every task, and changing environments will increase productivity. It is for this reason that companies are creating hybrid and open spaces that give employees different workspaces. This is also what co-working spaces do.

Changing environments will keep you fresh, productive and motivated and stop you from feeling caught in workdays that seem to go on and on in the same way.

Add a plant or a picture to your workspace, a whiteboard or some music. Make your workstation a nice place to be.

Sitting correctly

Being able to work anywhere you want can mean working in places that are not built for work. Some places can be bad for your back. According to the International Labour Office (ILO) 2017 report, 33% of people working from home experienced back pain, and nearly 50% experienced neck pain.[33] It is important to create a place where you can do your work in a comfortable way.

This means that the top line of your screen should be at the same height as your eyes and about half a metre from your face. It is also a good idea to buy a comfortable chair that you can change the position of, on wheels so you can easily move it. Sit–stand desks are becoming easier and cheaper to buy, too.

Try furniture in a specialist shop, and choose according to your space, work and needs. You can buy used furniture in markets or from some companies. You could also ask your employer to buy you the right furniture.

Another place where you can find yourself sitting badly is in a café. While the food and drink might be good, and there could be free WiFi, the seats are not usually designed for people to sit on for long or for working. They could be uncomfortable and give you a bad back. Plan your time in the café so you can have that nice coffee and cake while you answer your emails, then go back to work where you have your comfortable chair.

Keeping active

Sitting down too much is probably the problem most of us have in work today. Are you in front of the computer all day? Having a co-working space you cycle or walk to is a good way to start and end the day. If you are working from home, leave the house, go out and do something, even if you plan to come back soon. This will stop you going crazy.

In an office setting, it is normal to get up to get a drink, but in a remote work setting people can feel bad if they are not online for five minutes. Going to get a glass of water or some fruit, making a cup of tea or coffee is very good for giving you a break from the screen. It also brings in light exercise to your day.

Try to take some exercise during the day:
- A walk. You could set yourself a goal. 5,000 steps?
- An exercise group in a gym or park near you.
- A swim if there is a pool near you.
- A bike ride if you have a nice path, and the sun is out.
- If you are new to running, you could try building to 5 kilometres.
- If you already run, you could set yourself a goal to run 10 kilometres faster.

You can plan these activities with friends so that you see people outside your home through your day.

If you exercise often, it keeps you healthy, and it also helps you to concentrate better on your work, stops you from feeling stressed and increases productivity. A survey in the *International Journal of Workplace Health Management* showed that workday exercise gave people greater wellbeing, with 72% reporting that their time management was better, and they completed more work on days they exercised.[34] Many companies have seen how much more productive their employees can be if they exercise during the workday. Companies like Google and Lone have office gyms with yoga classes.[35] Remote companies are changing, too, by inviting their employees to take online classes or to join gyms.

Organizing and planning your day

To help you stay motivated, organize your goals into three groups: Work, Yourself and Home, with weekly, monthly and every three-monthly goals. Practise something called time-blocking on your calendar. This helps you decide which task to do when and allows time for things that are important, for work or for yourself.

This system allows you to do deep work, makes you understand how you spend your time, and also helps you measure the time needed for future work. The two most used time-blocking systems are: task-batching or day-theming.

Task-batching is putting tasks that are like each other together to do at one time. It helps you manage urgent daily tasks. For example, every weekday morning:

- 9.00 to 10.00: answering emails
- 10.00 to 11.00: call with the teams to check what they are doing
- 11.00 to 12.30: research

Day-theming is choosing one day to work on tasks with the same topics. For example:

- Monday: paperwork
- Tuesday: customer and project work
- Wednesday: training day
- Thursday: customer and project work
- Friday: research

For a remote worker, the best way to be as productive as possible is to put your work and home tasks into one calendar. Try the task-batching and day-theming systems and see which one works best for you, or mix both. You must be flexible and understand that sometimes plans need to change or you might need outside help.

Plan your days, check that you know when you are at your most productive, and do the tasks that you do better first. In his book *The 4-Hour Workweek*, Tim Ferriss shares many ideas on how to escape the nine-to-five workdays and live anywhere. He says that there is a big difference between being productive and being busy. He thinks you should concentrate on measuring your results by looking at the time spent, and find ways to stop doing less important tasks that take time. To do this, we should apply the 80/20 rule in all daily tasks. This rule says that 80% of results come from 20% of time and hard work. Decide on the tasks that you will not do and concentrate on what makes you productive and successful.[36]

Ending the working day

Some people may work from a co-working space and others fully from home, but for both you need a clear end to the day; it is as important as how you start it. When working in an office, travelling home is the natural break between home and workplace. When working remotely, you need to find a way of copying this.

Each person develops their own way, but the objective should be to look at the to-do list and plan for the next day. Knowing what you have to do first the next day will stop you feeling stressed. Leave your desk tidy so that you can start off fresh tomorrow.

Technology has made it easier for all employees, remote and not, to take their work everywhere, check their emails, answer messages and be ready to take a call, even on holiday. When you are remote, this can happen often and can become a negative part of your life because you do not leave your office desk at about the same time every day. Learning to switch off from work can really help your work–life balance. Finding it difficult to switch off after work is a big problem in remote working as it can make you ill.

Here are some things you can do to help your wellbeing:
- Use technology to tell yourself to take breaks often.
- Make time for exercise.
- Keep the same work and sleep hours.
- Leave your home sometimes. You need to do different things with different people.
- Learn to cook at home.
- Do not check **social media** during free time.
- Take holidays, and, where possible, switch off all technology.

CHAPTER NINE
Wellbeing

Wellbeing in practice

We researched how companies are practising wellbeing. Safeguard Global, an HR company in California, has over 500 workers across the world, 50% of whom are remote. It allows all its employees (and their families) to use an employee help program that looks at work–life balance. This program, which is private and different for every person, is delivered through a web application. It gives employees the chance to talk to specialists about family wellbeing, staying healthy, everyday life and work–life balance. It also gives employees help with **finances** or the law.

Global strongly believes that it should give employees help in their lives outside of work and often sends gifts to employees' homes to say thank you for work. Many companies do this. It is very important for remote workers because they are made to feel they are not alone or forgotten, but looked after.

Many companies with remote workers are looking into the wellbeing of their employees. They often choose an online company based in Madrid, ifeelonline.com. It has automated tools, chat messaging or video calls that people can use to get help.

Eating healthy food

Not having a daily structure will change your productivity and also what and when you decide to eat. On a good day, working remotely means being productive and going through eight hours of work without stopping, exercising in the morning and eating a healthy lunch. On a bad day, you do not get dressed all day, keep going to the fridge to find things to eat, and cannot concentrate on your work. You should remember that what you eat is important for productivity. Good food can increase the productivity of a country by about 20%.[37] You will be better able to concentrate and achieve tasks when you have eaten well.

Sleeping

Working remotely with people in different time zones can change the way you sleep. You may have to stay up late to connect with your colleagues and problems may worry you at night.

Only you know when you are most productive, so set yourself times to do things and do not change them. Have a work and a home phone and laptop, so you can switch off your work equipment, as you would when you leave the office. Your colleagues and customers will not look for an answer out of hours, but will often bring you into conversations that you can see when you are next online. Never check your work phone last thing at night or when you wake up. Start your day with some exercise, a shower and breakfast.

Taking time off

Remote workers usually take less time off than people in the office. Although 67% of remote companies offer more than four weeks' holiday every year, according to Buffer 2019 State of Remote Work report, remote workers take only two to three weeks.[38] Of course, some people probably make the most of the flexibility that remote work gives. It allows work while travelling, also known as a "workation". During a workation you can spend some time working, then have a swim at lunchtime and a nice walk on the beach after work, or a few runs down the mountain in the morning before switching on the laptop. While this can be great, it is not the same as switching everything off for a week.

People should take the full amount of holiday that a company allows them. It is very important to take days off, relax and spend time with family and friends, so that you stay productive.

CHAPTER TEN
Reaching out

Helping you to develop

According to the 2020 GitLab report, 24% of over 3,000 people who were interviewed believed they were in a worse position for their career when working at home and not with the rest of the team. They saw fewer chances to **progress** and develop their careers.[39]

If you are part of a team that has some remote workers, or you are working remotely with a team that is in an office, you may feel forgotten. To make people notice you more and to be a part of conversations, you need to follow a few easy steps:

- Take time before your meetings with your manager to list everything you have achieved, the problems you have faced and where you need extra help.
- Take an active part in conversations and meetings. If the technology fails in a meeting room, for example, if people cannot hear, it is fine to ask for the problem to be fixed, or the meeting room to be changed.

If nobody is listening to you or bringing you into conversations as a remote worker, you may want to look for a position in a company that does remote working well. But talk to somebody about the problem first. People in the office probably do not understand your situation as it does not touch them in the same way. In a fully remote team, you may find that your colleagues have the same problems.

For remote workers in co-working centres, there are great chances to **network**. Onlinemarketing.de shows that in a co-working centre you might meet people working in the same area. This can be good for your career. But you can also meet people working in different areas whose services you might need one day.[40]

Co-working centres have social events and talks by specialists. For example, Full Node in Berlin say their mission is "to increase the learning, social, and sharing value to their community through workshops, events, and **meetups**".[41]

There are also great chances to network online in events like virtual **conferences** and networking rooms where you can go and introduce yourself. Virtual conferences are good because you do not have to be in the same place to be a part of them, so you do not have to travel.

Developing a community

As a remote worker, there are plenty of ways to build or be part of a community of people like you. You could:
- join a co-working space in your area
- connect with specialist groups on social media (based on what they do or where they are), for example, on Facebook and LinkedIn
- go to in person events in your area like meetups or conferences that you might find interesting
- explore groups that do things you are interested in.

Remote working does not mean you have to be alone all the time. Joining a community will make you feel more connected, and it will also increase your social life. That kind of networking can be positive in developing your career.

Your two sides

Home is the safe space where you are with the people you care about. It is the place you return to after a day in the office. It is where you change into comfortable clothes and where you can be yourself. We all have our private side and our work side. Our private side is social, likes the people around us and needs to be liked by them. For the work side, it is more important to be good at what we do and for people to notice and respect us for that. These two sides of us can mix, for example, you can be social and friendly at work. But not much of the work you usually do comes into your home life. This all changes when you work remotely, when you have to bring the working you into the home, where you usually only find the private you.

When two people live together and both work from home, you should find ways to switch off and become private people again. Can you both switch off at the same time or is it confusing? Relationships can become difficult if you share a dining room or kitchen table as your remote office. You may love someone in your private life, but not understand them very well when they are working.

If there is enough space, each person should have an area they can call "the office". It could be an office in the garden or in the garage, or just some corners of rooms in the house. This allows each person to be themselves at work. Then meeting in the kitchen for lunch, they can become private people and be social and loving, and enjoy being with each other. This may not work for everyone, and perhaps more flexibility may be needed. For example, you could change the workspaces you create in the home from time to time. This will give you a break or make it fairer, if one space is smaller or colder than the other.

When you are interrupted

A positive thing about working remotely is that you are not interrupted by meetings or by colleagues talking to you. But other things can interrupt you, like people and pets you live with or housework. You need to manage this.

Housework

Keep your house or flat clean and tidy to create a nice environment to work in. One of the good things about working at home is that you can usually fit some housework into your workday, for example, doing the washing-up, putting clothes out to dry, or making lunch. It is OK to do it, but do not let it control your day.

Doing some small tasks around the house during the day gets you out of your chair and gives you a break. You could still be thinking about a work problem and suddenly have a creative moment! You could use jobs around the house to time your work.

Decide that you are going to complete a task by the time the washing is finished in the machine. This can train you to do deep work and be more productive.

With some organization and practice, fitting housework into your workday will become easier and you will quickly find out what works best for you. If not, then you might think of hiring some help. Think "Clean house = clean mind"!

People you live with

For most of us who work at home, there will be other people in the house when we are working, even if it is only for part of the time. You can make some rules for how you want people to communicate with you. This could be with messaging apps, so you can reply in your break. Set limits on when they can interrupt you and when they cannot. Sharing your calendar with the family will help with this, but you must also stay flexible and understand that you may be interrupted sometimes. Be polite and explain you want to finish something where possible.

If you have just become a parent, do not try to work and look after your children full-time; you will not do either very well. You might think that with your workplace at home, you can continue as before now that you have a baby. Everyone will be happy for you when you show the new baby during one of your video calls. But what will you do when the little one cries during a meeting and you have to leave a call early?

Older children should be taught the difference between wanting and needing your attention. You could try using a sign on your door saying when they can interrupt and when they cannot. Take short breaks with the children before they come looking for you. If it stops you from working, maybe think of hiring help during your busiest working hours.

CHAPTER ELEVEN
Finding balance

Work–life balance

It should be clear what work–life balance means: how you manage your own time for relationships, family responsibilities, outside interests, and time for work. But many people find it hard to get it right. It is important that you do not let work control you. As we have already discussed, you must carefully set limits around your working day.

It is important to remember the idea of balance. While you have home things you would like to do during working hours, you should think about what you need to do for work first. You may also sometimes have to change your own plans to fit around work. It is not good to take thirty minutes here and there for different little jobs and not find the time to do the work you missed. This is not balance. But if you have been working longer to finish an important task, then it is OK to finish a little earlier when you have completed it. This is balance.

It is possible to balance work and life, but you need to be careful that one does not control the other. If you have too much work, talk to your colleagues and your manager in your weekly meeting. If you are stressed at home, let your manager know that you have some problems. If you cannot find an answer, then you need to try to change the situation. For example, you might find somewhere for your children to go a few evenings a week after school to give you some time to get your work done. Or perhaps you could start an hour earlier so you can take time away from work, say, to take the children to football.

Feeling alone

Feeling alone is about missing people and social relationships. This can be a problem when working remotely. You might live alone, work alone and have all your shopping delivered. According to Buffer 2020 State of Remote Work report, 20% of those working remotely have problems because they feel alone.[42] Feeling alone and finding it difficult to communicate and collaborate with others are the greatest problems that remote workers face.

There are several things you can do about this. First, work in a co-working space where you have other people working around you. Try to build relationships with them by going to co-working events, or just start a conversation with the person next to you. You might be surprised that your co-workers are like you and have the same interests as you. They could tell you about things to do in the area or give you new connections or customers for your work.

Another way to stop feeling alone is by talking to family and friends on the phone or by video call every day.

It is important to talk to other team members and colleagues when you start feeling all alone. Telling them how you feel will help you to understand why you are feeling this way and what would make you feel better. Often, breaking with daily structures and fitting your day around what you need will help.

Feeling isolated

Feeling **isolated** at work happens when you are not in face-to-face contact with other team members. Feeling isolated can be more difficult to manage than feeling alone. Communication can be interrupted and lead to people on the team not being part of the conversation. It may just be that some of the team are working on a difficult problem and other team members are not included.

There are a few simple things you can do about feeling isolated. Speak to your manager, and explain that you are busy with your work but have no contact with the rest of the team. There should be meetings with the whole team, but maybe your manager stopped them, thinking that the team did not need them. You can explain that it is not true for you.

With hybrid teams where some are office based, or there is a group who all work in the same co-working centre, care must be taken to bring in the remote team members. This might be as simple as having short information meetings for a chat on a video call, or it might be that you need a calendar for meetings, with times for remote workers to meet the office-based or co-working team.

Being outside the office can also make you feel isolated when you do not have people you can ask for help, for example, to manage a technology problem, or give your work receipts to. A company can change this by having a "remote-first" rule, so that everyone puts their receipts in **digitally**. Or you can find a friendly IT person in the co-working space or, even better, your company's IT team can look at your laptop remotely.

A less clear side to being isolated is if you feel that your manager has not noticed your successes, or perhaps your career is developing more slowly than your colleagues'. You might need to communicate what you have achieved by describing what you have been doing for the team.

Burnout

According to Christina Maslach of the University of California, Berkeley, burnout is feeling stressed because, at the same time you are really tired from too much work, you are not connected to the job and not achieving any results.[43]

Remote workers are in greater danger of burnout than other workers because of their isolation. They are also in greater danger of feeling really tired because they are always trying to show their worth, which can stop them switching off from work.

It is important to look for signs of burnout, as your work may not be so good, but it can also come into other areas of family life and social relationships. This can be negative for your wellbeing.

If you feel stressed and tired, take a few days off and ask yourself whether you are feeling alone, not connected to people or if you have too much work to do. Talk about it, first with your close team and then with your manager, before getting more help if you need it.

Tired of video calls

There are several reasons why video calls make you tired. They make you think more about how you look to others and make you want to show people your best side. You have to concentrate more than you do in face-to-face conversations to read people's body language. Looking at a screen for a long time makes you tired, and having more people on the screen makes the problem worse.

To stop all these feelings, plan your video calls carefully and try to take breaks between calls. Do not have a full day of video calls if possible. Turn on video for meetings only if you need to, sometimes a phone call or email works just as well.

With six or fewer people, video can help people to talk to each other. For calls with more than six people, it is better not to have the video camera switched on and to turn the microphone off. Often these are meetings for giving information, so you do not need to speak.

Video calls usually last an hour because that was how long office meetings used to last, as people had to travel to get to the meeting, and it was polite to give them that time. Today, there is no reason why a video call cannot be just fifteen minutes long. If your call is not on video, think about doing "walking meetings". Research, in the *Harvard Business Review*, found that walking leads to an increase in creative thinking and keeps you active.[44]

Video calls have made people interested in the books that they can see in other people's bookcases. It is hard to read the titles of the books in a normal video call, although some are easier to guess from their covers. You can choose to say something about yourself through your books, or you can use a Zoom or Teams setting to cover them. Perhaps you can put this book in a good place so that people can see that you know what you are doing.

CONCLUSION
The future of remote working

Are we ready to go remote? Some people who have experienced remote working on the kitchen table, or in a small guest room quickly turned into a home office, may be less sure. Those who have tried a badly designed co-working space or tried to work in a noisy café will also be unsure. Small changes, the right technology and more experience with video calls will mean that more people will work remotely. Managers will understand that people can be trusted, as work continues to be delivered by a remote team.

What will make more companies have remote teams? As more people choose to work remotely, companies will want the best people. They will ask themselves why they are based in an expensive city and whether they need to have everyone in the office. Companies that allow people to work remotely will be in a good position.

Remote working allows people to choose where they live first, and then where they work. It will be important for towns and cities to have co-working centres. But there are two problems with these. We know that big, open offices are not the best design for this type of work. And who will pay for the co-working centres? Remote workers can decide to work at home for free, and limited social contact is seen as a small price to pay. However, if the company offered to pay part of the cost of the co-working centre, then the situation would change. Co-working centres would start to open in smaller cities, towns and even villages.

What might future technology allow us to do? Virtual Reality and Augmented Reality technology, which make our experience of the digital world more real, have been around for a while. But they have not been used to make video calling more like in-person meetings. The big question is whether they would be the answer to a problem, or whether better video conferencing and messaging will be enough.

There is another system being developed at the same time as remote working, called decentralized autonomous organizations (DAO). These organizations are linked to technology, that is not controlled by any centre, with easy-to-use programs. They are only just developing, but it is happening quickly. These experiments are leading to some interesting ideas and **innovations**.

How does this link to remote working? In some ways, organizations that try to structure themselves as totally remote are decentralized, without a centre. As the DAOs develop, and there are organizations that work well without having a centre, this could lead to remotely organized companies thinking more about how they are structured and how they work.

The future is bright, and remote working will be the way most of us work.

During-reading questions

INTRODUCTION

1. According to a KBC Bank survey, what do people find different about working from home?
2. Which technologies make it easier to work remotely?

CHAPTER ONE

1. What is the difference between digital nomads and hommies?
2. Why is six the magic number for a remote team?

CHAPTER TWO

1. What three things can a manager do to communicate well when using chat applications?
2. What do you need for a good video call?

CHAPTER THREE

1. How can you have informal meetings when you work remotely?
2. What is good about co-working spaces?

CHAPTER FOUR

1. What are the differences between an office-based manager and a remote manager?
2. What are the five types of manager–employee conversations that help a remote team to work well?

CHAPTER FIVE

1. What is an aligned team?
2. What is accountability, and how does it work in a remote setting?

CHAPTER SIX

1. How can you help improve asynchronous decision-making?
2. What do mediators in conflict situations at work need?

CHAPTER SEVEN

1. Why is behavioural-based interviewing important when building a remote team?
2. Why is pay for remote workers a difficult topic?

CHAPTER EIGHT

1. Where should you create a workspace if you are working from home?
2. How should you organize your goals to help you stay motivated when working remotely?

CHAPTER NINE

1. How can eating, sleeping and taking time off change the way you work?
2. What is the difference between a vacation and a "workation"?

CHAPTER TEN

1. How can you develop a community as a remote worker?
2. What are your two sides, and what problems can they give you as a remote worker?

CHAPTER ELEVEN

1. What is the difference between feeling alone and feeling isolated, and which is the bigger problem for remote workers?
2. What is burnout?

CONCLUSION

1 What will make more companies have remote teams?
2 What is the problem with co-working centres?

After-reading questions

1 Do you think we really need to be in an office? Why/Why not?

2 What do you think is the most important part of self-care for remote workers?

3 Which types of companies are ready/not ready to go remote, do you think? Why/Why not?

4 What would be more important to you: choosing when, where and how to work; or travelling to an office every day and working with other people face to face?
Give your reasons.

Exercises

INTRODUCTION

1 Are these sentences *true* or *false*? Write the correct answers in your notebook.

1 Different groups are treated more fairly when working remotely. ..*true*....
2 It is bad for workers to see company managers in their homes on a video call.
3 Workers around the world lose about a month of each year travelling to and from work.
4 In the last thirty years, offices have become smaller, more closed and more productive.
5 We probably send messages just as often as we walk over to a colleague's desk now.
6 Employers can now hire people from anywhere they choose.

CHAPTERS ONE AND TWO

2 Match the words with their definitions in your notebook.
Example: 1 – b

1 agenda
2 specialist
3 feedback
4 calendar
5 minutes

a a person who knows a lot about something and they give all their attention to it
b a list of things that people will discuss at a meeting
c when an employee writes down everything that is discussed and decided in a meeting
d a book or an app that shows the days, weeks and months of a year
e an opinion about something that can help you to make it better

CHAPTER THREE

3 **Match the verbs and the nouns together. Then write sentences in your notebook.**

Example: 1 – e <u>Co-working centres are good for building relationships.</u>

	Verb		*Noun*
1	build	a	career
2	create	b	idea
3	develop	c	research
4	share	d	networks
5	do	e	relationships

CHAPTER FOUR

4 **Match the two parts of these sentences in your notebook.**

Example: 1 – d

1 It is hard to notice when people have good or bad relationships

2 Virtual meetings can be difficult because you cannot see people's faces as well

3 Discussing expensive holidays or restaurants

4 Create a word that can be used to show people

a as you can during in-person meetings.

b might make some colleagues feel uncomfortable.

c that they are talking or acting in an incorrect way during meetings.

d when some are in the office and some are remote.

CHAPTER FIVE

5 **Write the correct word in your notebook.**
1. Employees have a lot of *independence* / independent, using their own abilities to reach goals in their own way.
2. Team **aligned** / **alignment** becomes even more important when you work remotely or as a hybrid.
3. **Accountable** / **Accountability** is the responsibility of each person to complete the task they have been given.
4. **Owning** / **Ownership** motivates the people in a team to think and find ways forward.
5. The way you measure **performance** / **performs** changes a little when teams are remote.

CHAPTER SIX

6 **Put the words in brackets in the correct order to make sentences in your notebook.**
1. Programs can be used with any communication and (tool / management / project) in a company.
   Programs can be used with any communication and project management tool in a company.
2. If a worker feels able to ask for mediation, it is a sign of a (company / culture / healthy).
3. There should be (channels / communication / good / of) to find (for / problems / quick / resolutions).
4. Arguing in person is rare in the (working / setting / remote).
5. Remote workers should have the same type of (systems / development / career) as office-based workers.

CHAPTER SEVEN

7 Put these actions in the correct order in your notebook.

a .... applying for a job
b ..*1*.. company branding
c .... hiring employees
d .... interviewing
e .... offboarding
f .... onboarding

CHAPTERS EIGHT AND NINE

8 Complete the table using the advice from the box.

> try day-theming try task-batching
> switch everything off for a week leave your home sometimes
> change environments learn to cook at home
> take the full amount of holiday
> set yourself a goal of 5,000 steps add a plant or a picture
> join an exercise group

organizing your day	*try day-theming*	*try task-batching*
ending your working day		
keeping active		
taking time off		
your workspace		

CHAPTERS TEN TO CONCLUSION

9 **Write the correct verb form, *present perfect* or *present perfect continuous*, in your notebook.**

1 Take time before your meetings with your manager to list the problems you ...*have faced*... (**face**) and where you need extra help.

2 As we .... (**discuss**), you must carefully set limits around your working day.

3 If you .... (**work**) longer to finish an important task, then it is OK to finish a little earlier when you .... (**complete**) it.

4 You might need to communicate what you .... (**achieve**) by describing what you .... (**do**) to the team.

5 Virtual Reality and Augmented Reality technology .... (**be**) around for a while, but they .... (**not use**) to make video calling more like in-person meetings.

Project work

1 Answer the questions at the beginning of Chapter Eight about how you work or study. Think about how you can improve your situation.

2 Design your own co-working space. Think about:
   - where it is (in a city, town, in the country, near a beach, etc.)
   - how it is organized (rooms, offices, open spaces, etc.)
   - when it is open and closed (days, times)
   - what type of work you can do in it
   - what technology or equipment it has
   - what non-work activities there are in the co-working space.

3 a Write an advert for a remote job. Say:
   - what the job is
   - how the employee will work
   - who the employee will work with
   - what type of person you need to be to do the job.
   b Write a letter applying for the job.

Glossary

accountable (adj.);
accountability (n.)
When someone is *accountable* for a *task*, they are *responsible* for it – they must do it and look after it. *Accountability* is the noun of *accountable*.

agenda (n.)
a list of things that people will discuss at a meeting

aligned (adj.); **alignment** (n.)
When people are *aligned*, they agree with each other and want the same thing. *Alignment* is the noun of *align*.

application (n.); **app** (n.)
An *application* is a computer program that helps you to do things. You usually call this an *app* when it is on your phone.

apply (v.)
If you *apply* for something, you write to ask if you can do or have it. People *apply* for jobs.

assess (v.); **assessment** (n.)
If you *assess* something, you think about it carefully and decide how good it is. *Assessment* is the noun of *assess*.

automated (adj.)
If something is *automated*, it is done by machines and not by people.

based (adj.)
used with the name of a place to say that something happens or someone works in that place

behaviour (n.); **behavioural** (adj.)
Someone's *behaviour* is what they do and how they do it. *Behavioural* studies look at people's *behaviour*.

branding (n.)
the types of advertising a company uses to make people remember a *product*

break (n.)
a short amount of time when you stop working and rest

calendar (n.)
a book or an *app* that shows the days, weeks and months of a year. You write the things you plan to do on a *calendar*.

career (n.)
the most important job or jobs you do through your life

channel (n.)
part of an *app*. You use a *channel* for sending and receiving messages between people about a topic.

chat (n. and v.)
Chat is messages that are sent between people online. People *chat* when they write messages to each other online.

cloud (n.)
a place to store information (= keeping it safe) so that it can be *delivered* to someone's computer or phone when they need it

coaching (n.); **coach** (n.)
Coaching is a way of helping someone to develop their abilities in their work or in their life. A *coach* is someone who helps people in this way.

co-living (n.)
living in a house with several other people, often sharing a living room and a kitchen

collaborative (adj.); **collaborate** (v.); **collaboration** (n.)
Collaborative work is when people work together to complete a job. They *collaborate* when they work together like this. *Collaboration* is the noun of *collaborate*.

colleague (n.)
a person you work with

communicate (v.); **communication** (n.)
You *communicate* when you share information with another person. *Communication* is the noun of *communicate*.

community (n.)
a group of people who are all the same in some way, for example, they believe the same things or they share the same interests

concentrate (v.); **concentration** (n.)
to give all your attention to the thing you are doing. *Concentration* is the noun of *concentrate*.

conference (n.)
a time when people in the same area of work or study meet, either online or in real life, to discuss important topics. A *conference* often lasts a few days.

conflict (n.)
when people argue because they want different things at the same time

connected (adj.); **connection** (n.)
You feel *connected* to a place when you have a strong feeling that you belong there. *Connection* is the noun of *connected*.

coronavirus pandemic (n.); **COVID-19 pandemic** (n.)
Coronavirus, or *COVID-19*, is an illness that makes people have problems breathing. A *pandemic* is when an illness affects many people across a whole country or the whole world. Millions of people died in the *COVID-19 pandemic* in the first part of the 2020s.

co-working (n.)
sharing a building and office *equipment* with other people who work for themselves or for different companies

create (v.); **creative** (adj.); **creativity** (n.)
If you *create* something, you make a new thing. *Creative* work is work where people have lots of new ideas and are good at *creating* things from them. *Creativity* is the noun of *create*.

cultural (adj.); **culture** (n.)
Cultural differences are the ways that groups of people in different countries or businesses usually behave, and the things they believe in. This is their *culture*.

dashboard (n.)
an area on a wall in an office, or a page on a website, where people can see information about the company's goals, successes, plans, etc.

decision (n.)
When you decide something, you make a *decision*.

deliver (v.)
to take something to a person or place

design (n. and v.); **designer** (n.)
Design (uncountable) is when you think about how to make something, how it will work and what it will look like. A *designer* makes *designs* (countable).

development (n.)
the different ways that an idea or thing changes and grows

digital (adj.); **digitally** (adv.)
Digital means using computers and the internet. If you do something *digitally*, you do it using computers and the internet.

disability (n.)
a problem with someone's body that makes it difficult for them to do things that other people can do, like walk or see

emoji (n.)
a small picture of a face or an object that you use in *digital* messages to show how you are feeling

employee (n.)
someone who is paid to work for a company or a person

equipment (n.)
all the machines and other things that you need to do a job

feedback (n.)
an opinion about something that can help you to make it better

finance (n.); **financial** (adj.)
Finance is the money that a company or person has. *Financial* means of or about money.

flexible (adj.); **flexibility** (n.); **flexibly** (adv.)
If you are *flexible*, you are able to change easily to fit the situation. If an *employee* works *flexibly*, they work at a time and in a place that fits their situation. *Flexibility* is the noun of *flexible*.

hire (v.)
to give someone a job at a company

human resources (n.)
the part of a company that is *responsible* for employment, keeps information about *employees* and helps them with problems

hybrid (adj.)
using two or more different ways of doing something

improve (v.); **improvement** (n.)
You *improve* when you become better. *Improvement* is the noun of *improve*.

independent (adj.); **independence** (n.)
If people are *independent*, they can choose what to do and how to do it. The noun of *independent* is *independence*.

innovative (adj.); **innovation** (n.)
If someone or something is *innovative*, they are good at *creating* or using new ideas, *processes* or *systems*. An *innovation* is a new idea, *process* or *system*.

instant (adj.)
Something that is *instant* happens immediately.

interview (n. and v.)
when someone asks you a lot of questions to decide if you will get a job. If you *interview* someone, you ask them questions to decide if they will get a job.

isolated (adj.)
If you feel *isolated*, you are not happy because you do not have much contact with other people.

key (adj.); **key performance indicator** (**KPI**) (n.)
Key means important. A *key performance indicator* is a way of *measuring* how well a company, *employee*, etc. has achieved its goals or *objectives*.

laptop (n.)
a small computer with a part that you can close to cover it. You can carry a *laptop* in your bag.

limit (n. and v.); **limited** (adj.)
A *limit* is a point where something stops being possible. If you *limit* something, you stop it from getting bigger or better. If you are *limited*, you are not able to go beyond a *limit*.

link (n.)
A *link* joins people or things together, often *digitally*.

list (n. and v.)
A *list* is words, names or numbers that have been written one below the other. If you *list* information, you write words, names or numbers one below the other.

marketing (n.); **market** (v.)
Marketing is the ways that a company tries to get people to buy the things it makes, for example, by advertising them and making *brands*. When a company *markets* its *products*, it does this.

measure (v.)
to find the size, amount, speed or weight of something. If you *measure* a company's or an *employee's* success, you decide how well they have done or *performed*.

mediation (n.); **mediator** (n.)
Mediation is when you try to end problems or *conflict* between two people or groups. A person who does this is called a *mediator*.

meetup (n.)
an occasion when people come to a place to spend time together

microphone (n.)
You speak into a *microphone* so that people in another place can hear you.

minutes (n.)
If you take the *minutes* at a meeting, you write down everything that is discussed and decided.

motivate (v.); **motivation** (n.)
To *motivate* someone is to make them want to do or achieve something. *Motivation* is the feeling of wanting to do or achieve something.

network (n. and v.)
A *network* is a group of people who work together. When people *network*, they meet and talk to other people about their business.

objective (n.)
something that you plan to achieve, especially in business

organization (n.); **organize** (v.); **organized** (adj.); **organizational** (adj.)
An *organization* is a group of people who work together because they want to do something. For example, a company is an *organization*. To *organize* something is to plan it and make it happen. If you are *organized*, you plan things carefully.

owner (n.); **ownership** (n.)
An *owner* is a person who owns something or who is *responsible* for something. *Ownership* is when you take *responsibility* for the things that happen in your life.

perform (v.); **performance** (n.)
How you *perform*, or your *performance*, is how well or badly you do something. In the *workplace*, a high-*performing team* works well together and achieves its goals.

process (v. and n.)
A *process* is a group of things that happen one after the other and cause a change or result. If you *process* documents, you do something with them so that something can happen. If you *process* information, you put it into a computer in order to *organize* it.

product (n.); **productivity** (n.); **productive** (adj.)
Product (uncountable) is all the things a company makes to sell. People buy and use a lot of different *products* (countable). If an *employee* is *productive*, they work hard and achieve a lot. *Productivity* is the amount of work *employees* do and how much they achieve.

progress (n. and v.)
When you make *progress*, you start to achieve your goals or *objectives*. You *progress* when you do this.

project (n.);
project management (n.)
A *project* is something you are trying to do or make. *Project management* is planning and *organizing projects*.

race (n.)
Someone's *race* is their family history or their skin colour, for example.

relationship (n.)
the way people are when they are together. If they like each other and work well together, they have a good *relationship*. If they do not like each other and work badly together, they have a bad *relationship*.

remote (adj.); **remotely** (adv.)
Working *remotely* means working far away from a place. *Remote* working is when an *employee* works from home and *communicates* with *colleagues* and customers *digitally*.

research (n. and v.)
Research is a way of learning about something by asking questions and finding information. You *research* a topic when you try to find information about it online.

resolution (n.)
You find a *resolution* when you find a way for people to agree, or when you find an answer to a problem.

respect (n. and v.)
If you *respect* someone, you treat them in a polite and kind way. When you do this, you show them *respect*.

responsible (adj.);
responsibility (n.)
If you are *responsible* for something, or if it is your *responsibility*, you must do it or look after it.

rule (n.)
something that you must or must not do

screen (n.)
the flat part of a television, computer or phone where you see the pictures or words

service (n.)
A *service* is something that helps you to do something, for example, ordering food or sending messages. An *organization* that offers *services* offers things you can use, for example, work, help or advice.

session (n.)
an amount of time that people use for an activity

setting (n.); **set** (v.)
1) A *setting* is where something is, and all the things, people and feelings that are part of that place.
2) A *setting* is the part of an *app* or mobile phone where you can *set* it to do something, for example, to make a particular sound. You *set* your phone or computer to do something, for example, to make a sound when a text message arrives.

social (adj.); **social distancing** (n.); **social media** (n.)
Social matters are the things that people do away from work and the way they live together. *Social distancing* means not being too close to other people so that you don't give each other an illness, for example *COVID-19*. *Social media* is websites like Facebook and Twitter.

space (n.)
an area where something happens

specialize (v.); **specialist** (n.)
If a person or *organization specializes* in something, they know a lot about it and they give all their attention to it. A *specialist* is a person who does this.

stressed (adj.); **stress** (n.)
If you feel *stressed*, you are worried because of problems in your life or because you have too much to do. *Stress* is this feeling.

structure (n. and v.)
Structure is the way in which something is *organized*. Something that is *structured* in a certain way is *organized* in that way.

survey (n.)
a group of questions that you ask a lot of people. You do a *survey* to collect information about what people do or think.

system (n.)
a way of working or doing something that is planned or has *rules*

task (n.)
something that you have to do, for example, a piece of work

tax (n.)
the money that people or *organizations* have to give to the government (= the people who control their country)

team (n.)
a group of people who are working together

time zone (n.)
one of the areas in the world where everyone uses the same time. For example, it might be midnight in London, and seven o'clock in the evening in New York.

tool (n.)
something that you use to help you do a job

track (v.)
to follow the *development* or *progress* of something

value (n. and v.)
A person's or an *organization's values* are the things they believe which affect their *behaviour*. If you *value* someone or something, they are important to you.

virtual (adj.); **virtually** (adv.)
Virtual activities are done on computers using the internet. If you do something *virtually*, you do it in this way.

wellbeing (n.)
Your *wellbeing* is your health and happiness.

workplace (n.)
the area or building where you work

workshop (n.)
when people meet to learn about something by discussing things and doing activities together

workspace (n.)
the part of the office – often a desk, or *virtual* place – where you work

References

[1] https://www.flexjobs.com/blog/post/flexjobs-2018-annual-survey-workers-believe-flexible-remote-job-can-help-savemoney-reduce-stress-more/
p141, Intro 1

[2] https://www.ilo.org/wcmsp5/groups/public/--- dgreports/---dcomm/---publ/documents/publication/wcms 544138.pdf
p141, Intro 3

[3] https://www.marketwatch.com/story/heres-how-much-your-company-pays-to-rent-office-space-2015-05-27
p141, Intro 4

[4] https://www.flexjobs.com/blog/post/big-numbers-the-environmental-savings-from-telecommuting/
p141, Intro 7

[5] The United Nations Economic and Social Council, 2018
p xii introduction

[6] https://www.fastcompany.com/90285582/everyone-hates-open-plan-offices-heres-why-they-still-exist;

https://www.forbes.com/sites/jiawertz/2019/06/30/ open-plan-workspaces-lower-productivit-employee-morale#56bfa49261cd;

https://royalsocietypublishing.org/doi/full/10.1098/rstb.2017.0239

[7] http://assets.regus.com/pdfs/iwg-workplace-survey/iwg-workplace-survey-2019.pdf
p141, Chapter 1, 1

[8] https://www.case1euro.it/
p142, Chapter 1, 3

[9] https://blog.hubspot.com/marketing/inspiring-company-mission-statements
p142, Chapter 1, 5

[10] https://www.clifbar.com/who-we-are/
p142, Chapter 1, 7

[11] https://www.glassdoor.com/employers/blog/diversity/
p142, Chapter 1, 10

[12] http://knowledge.wharton.upenn.edu/article/is-your-team-too-big-too-small-whats-the-right-number-2/
p142, Chapter 1, 14

[13] https://www.sciencedirect.com/science/article/abs/pii/002210317490033X
p142, Chapter 1, 15

[14] https://www.theguardian.com/technology/2018/apr/24/the-two-pizza-rule-and-the-secret-of-amazons-success
p142, Chapter 1, 17

[15] https://hbr.org/2016/01/collaborative-overload
p142, Chapter 2, 2

[16] https://www.standard.co.uk/tech/slack-london-data-lockdown-connecta4479976.html
p 142, Chapter 2, 3

[17] https://www.calnewport.com/books/deep-work/
p142, Chapter 2, 5

[18] Csikszentmihalyi, Mihaly (1996), *Creativity: Flow and the Psychology of Discovery and Invention*, New York, NY: Harper Perennial
p143, Chapter 2, 7

[19] https://doist.com/blog/asynchronous-communication/
p143, Chapter 2, 9

[20] https://remotehub.io/remote-companies-with-company-retreats
p143, Chapter 3, 3

[21] https://www.gallup.com/workplace/268076/manage-loneliness-isolation-remote-workers.aspx
p143, Chapter 5, 1

[22] https://basecamp.com/guides/how-we-communicate
p143, Chapter 5, 2

[23] https://blog.rechargepayments.com/how-to-thrive-as-a-fully-remote-company/
p144, Chapter 9,1

[24] https://research.tilburguniversity.edu/en/publications/moving-from-individual-to-constructive-accountability
p144, Chapter 9, 2

[25] http://opensource.guide/starting-a-project/
p144, Chapter 11, 1

[26] https://www.nytimes.com/2006/09/24/books/chapters/0924-1st-peas.html
p144, Chapter 12,1

[27] https://www.owllabs.com/state-of-remote-work
p145, Chapter 14, 1

[28] https://www.glassdoor.com/employers/blog/6-hr-recruiting-stats-you-need-to-know-for-2018-and-beyond/
p145, Chapter 14, 2

[29] https://toggl.com/track/out-of-office-building-a-team/
p145, Chapter 14, 3

[30] https://buffer.com/state-of-remote-work-2019
p145, Chapter 15, 1

[31] https://www.kentucky.com/news/business/article211602939.html
p145, Chapter 15, 3

[32] https://www.businessinsider.com/productivity-hack-working-from-home-2017-6
p145, Chapter 15, 4

[33] https://www.ilo.org/wcmsp5/groups/public/--- dgreports/---dcomm/—publ/documents/publication/wcms_544138.pdf
p145, Chapter 15, 5

[34] https://www.emerald.com/insight/content/doi/10.1108/1753835 0810926534/full/html
p145, Chapter 15, 6

[35] https://smallbusiness.chron.com/yoga-classes-workplace-1346.html
p145, Chapter 15, 7

[36] Ferriss, Timothy (2007), *The 4-hour Work Week: Escape 9–5, Live Anywhere, and Join the New Rich*, New York, NY: Crown Publishers
p145, Chapter 15, 10

[37] https://mindflash.com/blog/does-the-food-we-eat-affect-our-productivity
p146, Chapter 17, 1

[38] https://buffer.com/state-of-remote-work/2019
p146, chapter 18, 1

[39] https://page.gitlab.com/rs/194-VVC-221/images/the-remote-workreport-by-gitlab.pdf
p146, Chapter 19, 1

[40] https://onlinemarketing.de/karriere/new-work/coworking-spaces-arbeitsplatz-flexibilitaet-inspiration-networking
p146, Chapter 19, 2

[41] https://www.fullnode.berlin/events/
p146, Chapter 19, 3

[42] https://buffer.com/state-of-remote-work-2020
p146, Chapter 24, 1

[43] https://www.ncbi.nlm.nih.gov/pmc/articles/PMC4911781/
p146, Chapter 24, 2

[44] https://hbr.org/2015/08/how-to-do-walking-meetings-right
p147, Chapter 25, 3

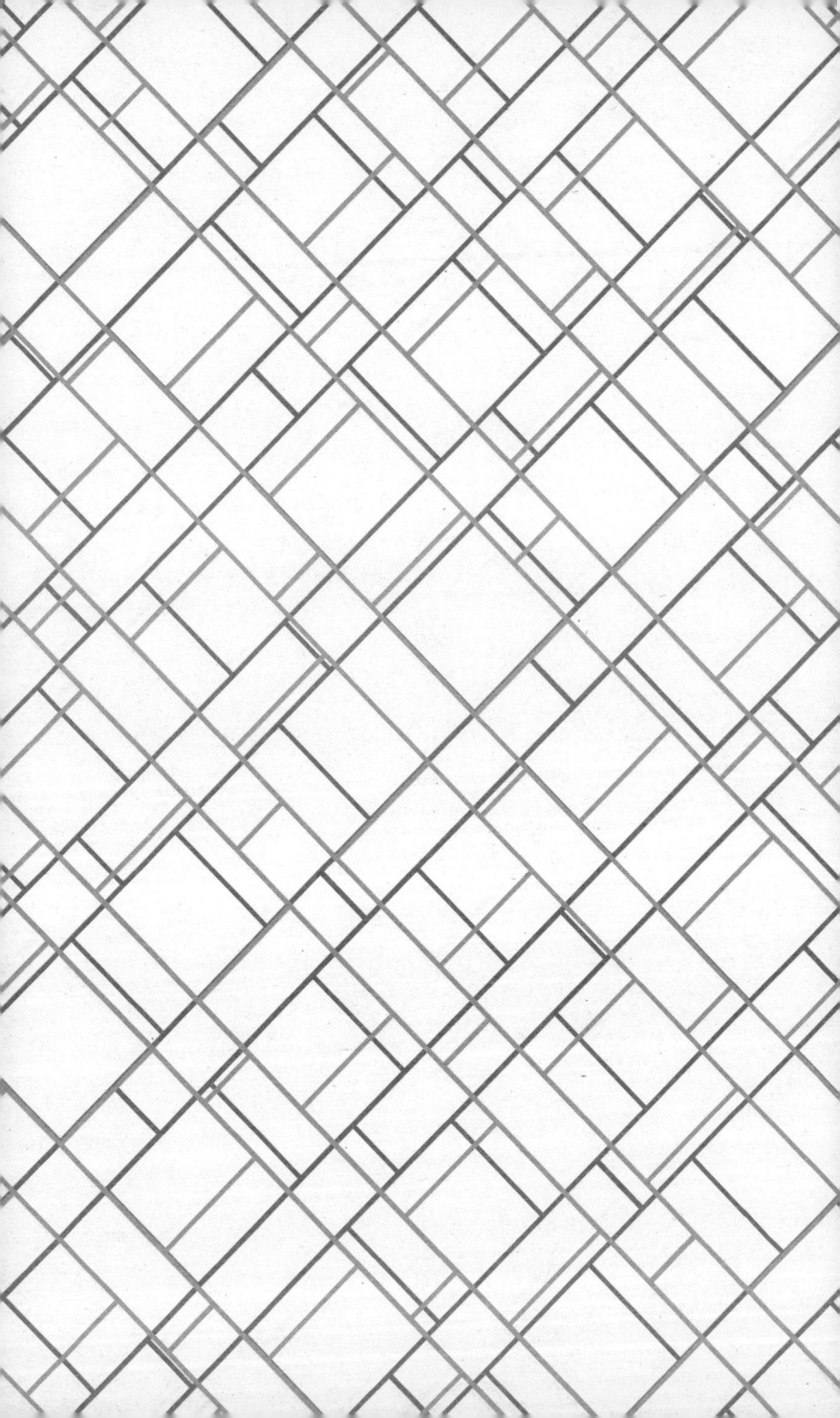

Penguin Readers

Visit **www.penguinreaders.co.uk**
for FREE Penguin Readers resources
and digital and audio versions of this book.